Advice for Working Moms

HBR WORKING PARENTS SERIES

*Tips, stories, and strategies for
the job that never ends.*

The **HBR Working Parents Series** supports readers as they anticipate challenges, learn how to advocate for themselves more effectively, juggle their impossible schedules, and find fulfillment at home and at work.

From classic issues such as work-life balance and making time for yourself to thorny challenges such as managing an urgent family crisis and the impact of parenting on your career, this series features the practical tips, strategies, and research you need to be—and feel—more effective at home and at work. Whether you're up with a newborn or touring universities with your teen, we've got what you need to make working parenthood work for you.

Books in the series include:

Advice for Working Dads

Advice for Working Moms

*Communicate Better with
Everyone*

Doing It All as a Solo Parent

Getting It All Done

Managing Your Career

*Succeeding as a First-Time
Parent*

Taking Care of Yourself

Two-Career Families

WORKING PARENTS

Tips, stories, and strategies for the job that never ends.

Advice for Working Moms

Harvard Business
Review Press
Boston, Massachusetts

Library of Congress Cataloging-in-Publication Data

Names: Harvard Business Review Press, author.
Title: Advice for working moms.
Other titles: HBR working parents series.
Description: Boston, Massachusetts : Harvard Business Review Press,
    [2021] | Series: HBR working parents series | Includes index.
Identifiers: LCCN 2020054363 (print) | LCCN 2020054364 (ebook) |
    ISBN 9781647820923 (paperback) | ISBN 9781647820930 (ebook)
Subjects: LCSH: Working mothers. | Parenting. | Work-life balance. | Sex
    discrimination in employment. | Sex discrimination against women.
Classification: LCC HQ759.48 .A385 2021 (print) | LCC HQ759.48
    (ebook) | DDC 306.874/3—dc23
LC record available at https://lccn.loc.gov/2020054363
LC ebook record available at https://lccn.loc.gov/2020054364

ISBN: 978-1-64782-092-3
eISBN: 978-1-64782-093-0

The paper used in this publication meets the requirements of the American National Standard for Permanence of Paper for Publications and Documents in Libraries and Archives Z39.48-1992.

CONTENTS

Section 2

Mommy-Tracked
Keep Your Career in Check

Section 3

Give Me a Break

Navigate Your Maternity Leave and Professional Breaks

Contents

Section 4

"A" for Effort

Handling Childcare and School Commitments

Section 5

Home Sweet Home
Managing the House and Family

Contents

Epilogue

Nobody's Perfect

INTRODUCTION

Managing the Working-Mom Job

by Daisy Dowling

"I'm covered in applesauce but making this happen!"

This statement of pride and resilience came from a mom I recently spoke with. As working mothers, we've all had these moments when everything may not go to plan, but we get it done. Yet most often in my coaching conversations with working mothers, I also hear about questions, doubts, stresses, and fears of various kinds.

I've come to think of it as "the pivot," the moment when an individual moves from telling me outward facts about themselves—their career accomplishments, tenure within their organizations, number of kids, their ages, and so forth—and about how they're "getting through," and begins talking about their real-deal thoughts and experiences. Some of it is logistical:

- Here's my to-do list—my main one. Then there are separate ones for all of the stuff I have to get done at work, at home, and with the kids. Sometimes I'll be driving and think of something that I've got to do, and I'm so worried that it will fall through the cracks that I'll pull over to jot it down.

- Growing up we used to sit down together for a real dinner each evening. Now, it's Takeout Central.

But for others, it's more emotional, questioning how they balance identity, perception, energy, and feelings:

- Am I supposed to tell clients about my kids, or hide the fact that I'm a mom? How much is it OK to bring people in?

- Sure, we've all got to cut out of work sometimes for the school event or because our kids are sick. But this is a tough environment, and I never want anyone to think that I'm taking it easy—or that I'm somehow "less than."

- I feel like I'm two people! At work I can act like, "I've got this"—completely capable. But that's not the "me" who the daycare center director pulls aside to talk about being on time for pickup.

These are all natural, normal experiences for *every* working parent. But many hardworking mothers face additional challenges and concerns. It's possible that your own mom didn't work when you were growing up, so the working-mom identity feels foreign to you. Maybe you're concerned about career advancement in a field that's historically male, or you're an expectant mom who's read recent news stories about how women often take on more of the day-to-day burden at home and want to strike that 50/50 split. Perhaps you're the overwhelmed mom of a teenager trying to figure out which of your "above and beyond" or extracurricular activities you can give up at work and still get promoted. Maybe the pandemic set you back or forced you to reconsider or recast the whole work-and-kids thing. If you did leave or lose a job, you may feel as if you're starting from scratch.

Let's be honest here: Even if things are going well, like so many other moms, you may worry that you're not proving yourself enough at work to advance your career and at the same time not spending enough time with your family. You feel as if everyone expects your full commitment: You've got to hand in the kids' medical forms on time, participate in school events, and take on stretch assignments or additional work travel. You may feel spread so thin that you ignore everything else—your friends, your health, and opportunities to volunteer for a charity you value—just to feel as if you're getting by.

As my conversation with any working mom continues, I'll often ask what kind of support she has or has reached out for. Most describe a patchwork of guidance from partners, fellow mothers at work, a mentor or two, an employee resource group, members of their community, or various role models. If you do rely on those resources, that's great; as both a coach and a full-time working mom myself, I know how empowering and effective it can be to look to the people in all parts of our lives, and to each other, for help and encouragement. In a demanding, complex situation like ours, those kinds of connections are essential. They work.

But sometimes finding this support is difficult. And even if we do have friends and family, most of us need something *more*—more practical, holistic, and basic. We need straightforward advice and information and timely, road-tested solutions that we can use today. We need a working-mom primer that we can personalize—a general how-to that we can each pull from, as we decide *what works for each of us.*

That's exactly what this book is. Whatever your unique working-mom story, whatever field you're in, however many years you're into this, and whether you're called mommy, mum, gramma, or something else, in the chapters that follow you'll find the broad-based, expert, and calm guidance you can use in combining career and kids. Let's say you have school-aged kids and are trying to tackle the challenge of working and parenting while also overseeing their education, extracurriculars, and meals; your children have left home, and you finally have time to give your career your full attention; or you're a first-time mother who's picked up this book because you're facing that all-important first day back after leave, feeling a little (OK, more than a little) nervous, and want to know how to make it all easier. Whether you're partnered or single, changing careers or going back to work after professional break, one of the few LGBTQIA+ moms in your organization, or simply want to step into working motherhood confidently and authentically, *Advice for Working Moms* will break down the most common problems you're facing and help you figure out a way through.

Each of these chapters was written because the issue it tackles—whether that's making your career more meaningful or getting food on the table—is one that many, if not all, working mothers struggle with. This book spans those concerns you have at work, at home, and in between, from how to think about backup childcare and how to manage as a dual-career couple to finding a family-friendly employer and explaining your family commitments to your boss. You'll read about ways to bring the working-mom guilt down to a manageable level, find the right support team to cart your kids from place to place—and simply make time for yourself. You'll even get some new perspective on the chores that take up so much of your valuable time at home and at work.

Take a look and find those challenges that speak to you right now. Dig into those chapters: Read these experts' practical ideas on how to make things work—and then take a step back and think about which of their recommendations are the most relevant and actionable in your own situation.

You may feel daunted or overwhelmed by the particular challenges called out here—and that's OK. We all do. As you use what you find in this book to build your working-mom skills and to get more comfortable and confident in your dual role, though—with how you want to combine children and career—something exciting will happen: You'll pivot again. You won't just look to other working-mom advisers, coaches, and role models. You'll become one.

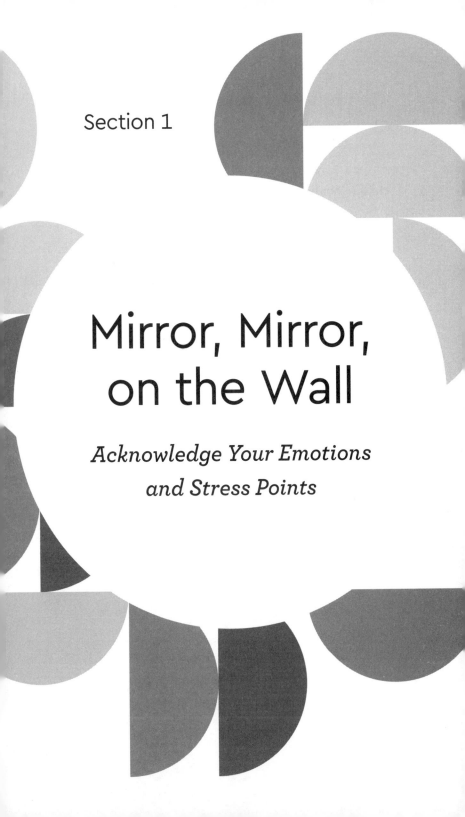

Section 1

Mirror, Mirror, on the Wall

*Acknowledge Your Emotions
and Stress Points*

Overwhelmed? How to Deal with "Doing It All"

by Daisy Dowling

Quick Takes

- Identify a clear goal for the future

- Align your time with your priorities

- Turn down tasks that don't contribute to your goal

- Keep a list of completed tasks

- Give yourself some downtime

*R*evise budget numbers. Parent-teacher conference Wednesday. Edit the marketing overview document. Finish summer camp applications. Give candidate interview feedback to HR. Grocery run—we're out of everything. Start drafting quarterly forecast. Call the roofer for the estimate. Organize team strategy session. Schedule kids' flu shots. Get back to Robin and Liu on IT plan. Get Tommy ready for math test tomorrow . . .

If you're a working mother, chances are excellent that at any given time, your to-do list looks like the one above—and that it stretches on, and on, and on—an endless, and eternally growing, list of deliverables. Is it any wonder research shows that most working parents feel stressed, tired, and rushed?[1] Or that when you look ahead, you feel more than a little overwhelmed?

As a responsible person and a hard worker, you know how to dig in and get things done. And since becoming a mom, you've tried various strategies to keep the ever-more-intense pace: moving paper to-do lists onto your smartphone, implementing new apps to track your tasks, spending more and more time logged into work each evening, cleaning up the endless queue of unread emails, sleeping progressively less each night.

Yet you're still haunted by the nagging sense of not getting enough done, of falling down in some way, of giving things that really matter short shrift—and feeling as if the wheels may come off the bus very, very soon.

The problem isn't in your organizational system or work ethic—it's in how human brains are wired. It's *normal* to feel overwhelmed with so much to do and so many demands on you.

But here's the good news: There are simple and effective techniques for taming the feeling of being overwhelmed—for getting *out* of it. These are things any working parent can do, starting *today*, to feel more competent, calm, and in control and to start shrinking that task list permanently. Here are four of the most powerful.

Know Your Endgame

Well-run organizations, and good managers within them, have a clear, compelling view of the future. They have a few strategic goals. They set revenue targets annually. They know what results will permit them to say, "We succeeded." With clarity on where they want to go, they have confidence in their decisions and take motivation from what lies ahead.

As a working mom, do you?

Most of us working mothers are focused on simply getting through the day, which (let's be real) is daunting.

Yet that very determination to hunker down and conquer today's task list makes working parenthood feel even more overwhelming and relentless. Your task list owns you, rather than the other way around. Over 18 years (or more) of working parenthood, constantly feeling "I have a million things to do today" will be pretty disempowering and exhausting.

By identifying the long-term, positive outcome of your working motherhood—by determining a specific picture of future success—you can begin to flip that equation. Knowing that your goal is to "serve as a vice president of this organization, while raising my children to be healthy, financially independent adults" provides a sense of self-determination, confidence, and motivation. *You* made the decision. The goal is reachable, and you can focus on the tasks that accrue toward it. Even on the busiest or worst of days, you have a fixed point on the horizon you're moving toward—and you'll know it when you get there.

To be clear: There is no "working-parent magic formula"—the definition of success is, and should be, different for everyone. "To lead this company as CEO, while partnering with my spouse to raise healthy, ethical kids" is just as valid as "to make enough money to cover my kids' expenses—while never missing family dinners." But by identifying a goal that is personal, positive, and future-framed and that covers what you want from your career and for your children, you move yourself away from feeling so frantic and toward being in the psychological driver's seat.

Invest Your Time Accordingly

Working parents who have a clear view of what they're working toward are more able to prune their calendars of commitments that don't align, and to spend time and energy on the things that matter and that provide real satisfaction.

If your goal is "become a partner at this firm, be known as a leader in my local professional community, and raise my kids into well-adjusted adults who remain connected to their religious heritage," then it's important to go the extra mile at work, attend industry conferences in your city, and take your kids to Sunday school. But representing your firm at an international conference or attending every single football game isn't, because they don't align with your goal.

With your working-parent vision clear, try spending 10 minutes each Friday doing a "forward calendar audit": Look over next week's calendar or to-do list, identify the items that don't fit with your goals, and commit to delegating or saying no to 5% of them. By making this a habit, over the course of the year you will be able to win back a significant amount of your own time and increase your sense of satisfaction and control.

Keep a "Got It Done" List

In the late 1920s, Russian psychologist Bluma Zeigarnik described what has since become known as the Zeigarnik Effect, which states that people remember, and fixate on, uncompleted or interrupted tasks significantly more than finished ones. It's why hearing a few seconds of a song on the radio can leave you humming all day, trying to remember how the song ends, and why many TV shows end each episode inconclusively, so you'll be left obsessing until you see how the plotline resolves.

Uncompleted tasks torture us: They take up all our mental space and create enormous emotional noise and tension; when we don't have closure, we get anxious. And for any working parent, with all the open items we have both at home and at work, that's a *lot* of anxiety. Your task list is necessary, but regardless of how and in what form you keep it, it won't help relieve this stress. If anything, it fuels it.

The effective short circuit is to keep a brief, informal list of *completed* (rather than undone) items, from both work and home. Write down this year's finished projects, problems solved, your wins—whatever "win" means for you. *Beat our quarterly numbers. Found Sasha a science tutor. Brought in the pharma account. Made it to Diego's baseball game last week.* Then look over this list and remind yourself of how much you've done—how much you've produced and accomplished, in both spheres.

My clients and coachees report that even a single minute spent doing this helps them feel significantly less frantic and overwhelmed. In the words of one of my clients, "It makes me feel like I'm winning."

Make a habit of looking at the list, push out some of that constant to-do noise with "already done" confidence, and you'll find yourself calmer and happier.

Schedule a Regular Power Outage

As a working mom, your to-do treadmill will never slow or stop, but you can choose to step off it, briefly.

Sometime in the next two days, set aside 20 minutes in which you turn off all devices, set aside your task list, and do nothing productive at all. Your job is simply to spend time in an activity you enjoy with your family. It could be eating dinner together, dancing the Hokey-Pokey with your toddler, or going on a jog with your teenage son. You're a high-powered person in a high-powered career, but for these 20 minutes, the power is out.

Even in such a short window of time, you'll find that your stress will decrease, and your feeling of "having done something positive for myself and my family" will go up. And even more important, during a crazy day, you'll regain a sense of agency: You've taken an affirmative decision to do this and made it happen on your own terms.

There's a reason so many major religions embrace the idea of a Sabbath, and why so many highly successful people make it a habit to take regular vacations: It works. Taking time to withdraw from the world and turn off from work centers us, making us more resilient and more productive. For working parents, finding meaningful flexibility and longer breaks can be hard. But even for the busiest of us, in the most demanding and time-pressed professions, 20 minutes off is doable.

Working motherhood is demanding. It requires one person to do two challenging jobs well, and in an always-on world. As in any extreme job, some degree of fatigue, stress, and self-doubt—of general feelings of being overwhelmed—is inevitable. But the more you can set your own course, make affirmative decisions aligned to it, have confidence in your performance, and enjoy yourself along the way, the better off you, your career, and your family will be.

Adapted from "How Working Parents Can Feel Less Overwhelmed and More in Control," on hbr.org, January 12, 2018 (product #H043WY).

Let Go of Working-Mom Guilt

by Sheryl G. Ziegler

Quick Takes

- Identify your values and priorities
- Ask for help, even if you feel vulnerable
- Redefine what you "should" be
- Stop comparing yourself to others

You wonder how some working mothers seem to be able to do it all—easily—while you struggle under the weight of work-life balance stress. You feel time running out to achieve your career aspirations while your kids are growing up so quickly. No matter where you are, you feel as if you should be elsewhere, getting something productive done. Secretly, you dream of a weekend away but come up with excuses about why you can't do it.

In her book *Forget Having It All*, author and journalist Amy Westervelt sums up the *working-mom dilemma*: "We expect women to work like they don't have children, and raise children as if they don't work." Because of this, women feel guilty—guilty for working and guilty for not. Blurred boundaries of work time spill into family time (and vice versa). Half listening to children's stories from their day or missing out on meaningful time with them can make mothers feel as if they are failing. It seems like a no-win situation, and it fuels feelings of being overwhelmed, exhausted, and defeated that can lead to burnout.

Working moms are chasing the balance of working a job that they want or need and being the mom that they envisioned. You don't just feel bad about letting your kids, team, or boss down; you also feel guilt about practicing self-care, remorse for not helping aging parents enough, or embarrassment about telling a friend how stressed out you are—as if you don't have a right to feel this way.

Letting go of this guilt should be at the top of your to-do list. My experience counseling working mothers has shown me that, while they do still feel stressors, they also experience significant relief when they are mindful and intentional about their mindset and behaviors. Here are some strategies to start freeing yourself of guilt.

Forgive Your Past Self

Letting go of guilt has to start with a commitment to stop beating yourself up over your choices and circumstances—particularly those that have already happened. Guilt gone awry turns into shame, and it is emotionally painful to constantly feel as if you are a bad mom, a bad employee, or a bad friend. Instead, remember the reasons behind your choices. Every time you think to yourself, "I feel bad about ___," replace that with, "I made that decision because ___." Acknowledge the reason behind the decision and then move forward with a clean slate.

Revisit Your Values

For years, I have worked with parents who experience guilt over their parenting decisions, their hours at the office, or the hours plugged into work at home. One of the most grounding exercises people can engage in is getting clear about what their values and priorities are in life and then living life in accordance with them. So often people say one thing matters to them most, but they don't live according to those values.

For instance, if family time is at the top of your list but you don't feel as if you get enough of it, consciously find ways to spend more time with your family. Practice saying no to unnecessary commitments, like volunteering at every school fundraiser, going to a regular happy hour with coworkers (even virtually), or sitting on your neighborhood HOA board. Involve your children in tasks you already do, like completing chores, making meals, or taking the dog for a walk. Or use your weekends intentionally, dedicating blocks of time for family, rather than errands. This will likely entail setting clear boundaries in other areas of your life and constantly revisiting (and updating) your family values statement so that you adhere to what you want.

Ask for Help

One of the hardest things for many women is to ask for help. Instead of requesting help, a working mom may just fuel her stress by trying to do it all herself—then realizing that it is just impossible. Asking for help takes practice, but once you take a vulnerable step in doing so, others around you will start doing the same. Reach out to neighbors, friends, parents of your kids' friends, your own parents, your in-laws, the aftercare program at school, or carpool parents. Before you know it, no one has to feel bad about asking, and it becomes a reciprocal relationship in which everyone benefits.

Be "Good Enough" at Home

The idea of the "good enough parent" goes back decades. Attachment researchers, including British psychologist John Bowlby, discovered that parents need to be emotionally present to comfort their child, attune to their child's feelings, show delight when seeing their child, and support their child in order to have a healthy and secure parent-child attachment.[1] In other words, they are caring for and connected with their child, without sacrificing their personal needs and health.

We need to follow this example and lower the bar from the perfect mom who can do it all, who does everything she should be doing, and is praised for her selflessness to the mother who reclaims her own life and takes care of herself. Rather than putting additional pressure on yourself, remember the basics. Focus on those ways you're already supporting and connecting with your children and allow yourself to simply be good enough.

Unfollow Those Who Bring You Down

Watching other people vacation, share their family photos, or publicize their latest promotion on social platforms like Facebook and Instagram is enough to drive a working mom to tears. The time you take to scroll on social media for connection is a time that needs to lift you up. If you find that a person's or group's posts consistently bring you down, unfollow them.

Last, remember that guilt is inherently tied to empathy. Feeling guilty means you have compassion, care, and concern for those around you. Getting rid of your guilt does not mean that you are not a loving or kind mother. It means that the empathy behind the guilt will be realized. Instead of feeling stuck, the power of compassion can motivate you to connect with your work as well as find the joy in being a mom.

Adapted from "How to Let Go of Working-Mom Guilt," on hbr.org, September 4, 2020 (product #H05TYV).

Understanding Identity as a (New) Working Mother

by Janna Koretz

Quick Takes

- Rethink how you define success

- Acknowledge that you're your own worst critic

- Celebrate your wins—both large and small

- Treat yourself with understanding and flexibility

arenthood changes you. The roles you used to play, the identities you used to claim—lawyer, dog lover, spin enthusiast—all come second to your new responsibilities. For some, this rearrangement of priorities can lead to a crisis of identity. This is especially true for women, who for both social and neurological reasons tend to feel the split demands of home and work most acutely.[1]

As a clinical psychologist focused on the mental health challenges of people in high-pressure careers, I often read articles and papers about how to get back to "feeling yourself" after becoming a parent. But there are no easy answers, no top 10 lists of tips and tricks that can bring instant comfort and clarity.

Rachel (name has been changed), a longtime therapy client of mine, was a successful trader who had—as far as I could tell—never failed at anything in her life. So, she never anticipated that being a working mother would be something she couldn't handle. Multitasking in a high-stress environment was basically her job description. How hard could it be to add on a few extra tasks at home?

But when Rachel returned to work after maternity leave, she felt as if she was floating, distracted. She couldn't perform to her own standards at the office and felt as if she was dropping the ball at home, too. She had built her identity around her competence and intelligence. Now that all seemed to belong to someone else.

Research into the neurobiology of motherhood has provided some hints about why new mothers often find the return to work so challenging. After giving birth, multiple neurological and structural changes occur that can make it difficult for the new mother to exactly replicate her previous functioning.[2] The brain actually redesigns itself, trimming old connections and building new ones. The result appears to be a brain optimized for "theory of mind"—the ability to understand what others might be thinking and perceiving.

These cognitive and perceptual superpowers helped keep our ancestors alive while living among woolly mammoths. They also give mothers that uncanny ability to analyze their new baby's cries and guess exactly what the infant needs. But the brain doesn't know about our modern work environment; those connections that got trimmed might have been the ones that you relied on to get your job done.

If you're someone who has constructed your adult identity around your career, suffering from "mommy brain" can shake your foundations. Even more unnerving, though, is the sudden instinct some feel to actually want to engage in motherhood above all else. The collision of these two identities, these two seemingly incompatible ways of being—that's the recipe for a good old identity crisis.

Losing your bearings like this isn't just uncomfortable. It can lead to anxiety, depression, burnout, relationship issues, and even substance use. And for most of my clients who are working parents, the chaotic shift to remote work in the time of Covid-19 made things even harder. The boundaries that they once could draw between the household and the office have been blurred, and the human relationships that once gave work meaning have been reduced to a matrix of disembodied, video-chatting heads. No wonder that so many of us feel so unlike ourselves.

Sorting out your identity can be a long and complicated endeavor, but there are two mental rethinks that I often use with my clients to help them figure out how to approach the complicated new world they find themselves in.

Rethink Success

You used to aim for maximum efficiency and effectiveness. Now, you can give yourself a gold star just for survival. You'll have to let a lot go and adjust your definition of success. I guarantee you'll come out ahead if you give yourself credit for all your work on the home front. To do so, try redefining success as getting stuff done both in and out of the office.

Where success might once have meant closing a big client over steaks at a swanky place downtown, it now might mean whipping up breakfast for dinner (ignoring the mess all over the house) as you shout silly songs to your kids giggling in the other room. That client might take an extra day or two to sign, but in the meantime, you've been racking up the wins at home. You're doing way better than you're giving yourself credit for—frame those parenting victories as something to be celebrated.

Rethink Yourself

Our identities go through many changes through the course of our lives. Instead of feeling that your identity has been disrupted, think of it as having been expanded. You were once yourself—now you're yourself, plus something else. There's room to become more.

Parenthood is far from the first time your identity has undergone a shift. Taking on big personal projects like training for a triathlon can often shift our perceptions of ourselves. In that way, adding "parent" to your identity shouldn't require you to abandon old parts of yourself, any more than adding "triathlete" or "great cook" or "photographer" should.

We're often our own most vicious critic. Let go of some of the pressure you're putting on yourself and treat yourself with the understanding and flexibility you'd grant to your best friend. Would you rip your friend for feeding their kids chicken nuggets two nights in a row because something came up at the office? You'd probably laugh about it with them, and then pass the ketchup.

Above all, realize that there are no easy answers, just the hard work in becoming a better (if more complicated) version of yourself. And after you help fight a worldwide pandemic by working from home, answering emails through a soupy brain fog while your toddler is screaming for mustard with their nuggets instead—you'll get there.

Adapted from "New Mothers, Let's Talk About Your Professional Identity Crisis," on hbr.org, August 19, 2020 (product #H05SWO).

Section 2

Mommy-Tracked

Keep Your Career in Check

How to Identify a Family-Friendly Employer

by Suzanne Brown

Quick Takes

- Identify what you want in an employer

- Talk to past employees in your network

- Ask about a typical day in your interviews

- Discuss flexibility and remote work

- Ask HR about benefits and support options

I f you're a working parent looking for a new job or interested in making a career move, your search might not only be about finding a great professional opportunity. You may also want a more family-friendly employer. If that's the case, it's helpful to get a more complete picture of work life at the potential employer *before* you come on board. Learning how the company has supported other parents will help you understand if its actions and culture align with what you want and need.

Before you even explore potential employers, identify what you're looking for. This gives you the lens through which you look at a job opening, so you can start to understand if this organization can give you the opportunity and lifestyle that you want. Think through the most important commitments you have with your family that might impact time at work, like eating dinner as a family each night, coaching your child's soccer team, or assisting with remote schoolwork. Consider what benefits you want from the employer and how important they are to you and your family. Reflect on how your current or previous employers have fallen short, to identify what was missing. It could also be helpful to visualize your ideal scenario as a working parent both today and long term as your kids get older or your family grows.

Then, as opportunities present themselves and you line up interviews, do your homework. You may feel limited, especially if you're stuck interviewing remotely or unable to see office culture firsthand, but you can find a lot of information—as well as ask a lot of questions—to find the right opportunity. Here's how.

Online Resources

Start with the company website. Review how the company talks about employees and what it shares regarding employee support. Creating an environment for working parents begins at the top. Look at senior leadership and the company's board of directors. Can you tell if they have families? Do they talk about a family-friendly environment? Are there women? If you're answering no to most of these questions, this may not be a family-friendly environment, especially at more senior levels, which could be a red flag for your long-term growth opportunities.

Look, too, for any information about employee resource groups (ERGs), paying special attention to those for working moms and dads. Review any public information on family leave, if a child were to become ill, a spouse or partner required assistance after an injury, or an aging parent needed care. Dig into any parental leave and programs offered to new moms, such as a part-time ramp-up or a work-from-home period, and see if they extend these options to new dads, as well.

Wherever the company features employees on the website, such as in published articles, on its blog, or in press releases, look for information on a typical day in the organization that suggests a reasonable work life, or signals that colleagues and the company as a whole have positively impacted employees' work life or family. (Accounting firm DHG, for instance, features such stories on its corporate blog.) Then, see how their stories compare to what else you find on the website.

Go outside the company's website, too. Do a quick online search for recent news, both good and bad. Read current and former employee reviews on places like Glassdoor and review top 100 lists in publications such as those published in *Working Mother*. And track down interviews with senior leaders to see what they share about their family life.

Personal Connections

In addition to online resources, tap into your network to get personal anecdotes about the company. You want to piece together a more complete picture of being a working parent with this employer. You might see warning signs or get ideas for questions to ask during interviews.

Use LinkedIn and Facebook to find friends, friends of friends, connections through your professional network, or school alumni who may be employed, or previously employed, by the company. Talk to them about company culture and probe about official policy versus reality. If these are former employees, don't be afraid to ask about why they left.

Talk to them about work-life balance failures, as well. Keep an ear out for statements like, "Too many moms are put on a 'mommy track'" or "All the working dads end up on the same team." Perhaps the company tried a program to support working parents, and it didn't work. What did the company learn? What can you uncover about why working parents leave? Is there a consistent pattern of working parents leaving because they lack support?

Interviews with Current Team Members

When you reach the interview stage, ask about the position in question, but also aim to find out more about the company and its culture. Consider who is interviewing you and listen closely to what they share. If all of your interviewers say they don't have a family or they have kids and a full-time, stay-at-home spouse or caretaker, this could be a red flag.

This is a great opportunity to hear about an average day, too. Pay attention to the length of a normal workday and if there are back-to-back meetings or video calls, all day, every day. This could hint at long hours or an expectation to work late nights or early mornings.

Another great topic to cover in your interviews is flexibility. Look for formal structures such as job shares, part-time options, split schedules, and day-to-day flexibility for when your child gets sick, has a school event, or requires your attention while you work from home. Covid-19 shifted how employers approach flexibility, especially remote work.[1] Ask about their experience during the pandemic. How did managers and the employer support employees who were supervising their children's distance learning or entertaining young children? Are flexibility and remote work now built into the work culture—or was that considered temporary? And remember that being family friendly extends beyond managing work life with your children. Find out how this employer supports families with aging parents and sick family members as well.

If you have specific questions about benefits, talk to your HR contact. Ask about the benefits and support structures for working parents. These benefits could include paying to transport milk for moms who pump while traveling or for backup childcare and elderly care.

And inquire about workplace wellness programs that help prevent things like burnout.

Choosing the right position is not only about checking the role for the right fit; you want the company to be the right fit, too. Tap into the many resources available early on and during the interview process to uncover red flags and do research to understand how work life will be with a new employer. There are many family-friendly organizations. Take the time to fully understand the opportunity on both professional and personal levels before you sign on.

Adapted from content posted on hbr.org, September 8, 2020 (product #H05UAQ).

How to Build a Meaningful Career

by Amy Gallo

Quick Takes

- Know what *meaningful* means to you
- Identify things you're good at and enjoy doing
- Consider your ideal salary, benefits, and schedule
- Imagine possible roles and create experiments to test them
- Think about where you want to be in 5, 10, 20 years
- Make a budget to give yourself a financial buffer

Everyone aspires to have purpose or meaning in their career, but when you have other obligations to consider, it's easy to let fulfillment in your job fall in the priority list. Still, building a career that helps you meet your family responsibilities *and* feeds your soul is not only possible, but important. So what practical steps can you take to make sure you're not just toiling away at your desk to make a paycheck, but you're doing something you genuinely care about?

What the Experts Say

Unfortunately, most of us don't know how to make the job decisions that lead to satisfaction. Nathaniel Koloc, founder of the talent consultancy and executive search firm Formidable, says that's because no one really ever teaches us how: "Very few parents, teachers, and mentors urge us to think about this or give us mental models to use," he says. "We tend to only get nibbles of what meaningful work is in our twenties." As a result, we often pick jobs for the wrong reasons, says Karen Dillon, coauthor of *How Will You Measure Your Life?* "We look for things that we're proud to talk about at a cocktail party or look good on a résumé." But rarely are those the things that translate to satisfaction.

Here are principles you can follow to find a career—and a specific job—you love that's not just good for you as a person, but as a parent, too.

Know what "meaningful" means to you

Am I respected by my colleagues? Am I being challenged? Am I growing? Do I believe in the mission? Am I proud of the work I do? "These are the things that are going to make the difference between being OK with your job and being truly happy," says Dillon. But "meaningful" means something different for each individual. "Don't just look to obvious things, like salary, title, or prestige of the company," says Dillon. Koloc identifies four categories to consider.

Legacy. This is about the concrete outcomes of your work. What do you want to achieve? Sure, you may spend a lot of your day responding to emails or attending meetings—most jobs entail at least some of that—but what evidence do you want of your work? What do you want to look back on and know you accomplished? What do you want your children to remember about the work you did? You might find it rewarding to advance the math skills of 80 students in one year, build six desalination plants over the course of your career, or start a small family business that you can leave to your children. This is often a question of how close to the front lines you want to be. Some people want to help sick people directly, while others aspire to help pass policies that will give large numbers of people access to health care.

Mastery. These are the strengths that you want to improve. For example, if you enjoy connecting with people, you could use that skill to be a psychologist or a marketer. Similarly, if you're a strong writer, you could use that skill to write fiction or copy for advertisements. The key is that you are using these strengths in a way that you find rewarding. "Being good at something you don't enjoy doesn't count," says Koloc. "It has to be something you love to do."

Freedom. This is about the salary, benefits, and flexibility you need to live the life you want. For some people, this may mean a high paycheck that allows you to take your family on vacations, to send your kids to summer camp, or to be able to afford music lessons for your children. For others, it could be the freedom to work when and where you choose. Many working parents want flexibility to take an hour or two during the workday to participate in a child's school event or to accompany an aging parent on a doctor's visit. Others want to know they can have dinner with their family every night or avoid working on the weekends. You need to know the lifestyle you want and ask whether your job is helping you fulfill that.

Alignment. This last category covers the culture and values of the place where you work. This is not the same as mission, warns Koloc, but is about whether you feel as if you belong. What are the beliefs and priorities of the company and the people you work with? How do people treat each other? Do colleagues eat lunch together? Discuss their families and personal lives? Are there other working parents there who you can turn to for support? "It's important to enjoy spending time with your colleagues and your manager," says Dillon. The content of these categories will vary by person. Dillon suggests making a list of all the things you value and then prioritizing them. This list will help guide your decisions and can be used to evaluate specific opportunities like a new assignment in your current role, a job at a different company, or a new career path.

Form hypotheses

If you're unsure what matters most to you, think through a given day or week at work. Ask yourself: What made me most happy on the job? What did I find most frustrating? Then, Koloc suggests, come up with a few hypotheses about what is most meaningful to you. *I want a job where I create something that people can use every day. I want a job that allows me enough flexibility to pick up my kids from school three days a week. I want a job where I'm directly interacting with people in need. I want a job that will make my teenagers proud of what I contribute to society.* "Be careful not to overcorrect for a particularly bad job experience," says Dillon. "When you have a micromanaging boss, for example, it's easy to think that your biggest priority is to work for a manager who doesn't smother you, but if you seek out that one thing, you may end up being unhappy for slightly different reasons."

Run experiments

Once you've nailed down your hypotheses, it's time to test them. There are a variety of ways to do this. First, you can try things out within an existing job. Take on a new assignment that allows you to try out new skills. "Look for opportunities to enhance your job. Sign up for a new cross-company initiative or propose taking something off your boss's plate," suggests Dillon. "I've never known many managers to say no to people offering to help out." That said, research shows that women often take on more office housework than men, so be sure that you're choosing work that adds value to the organization and that you get credit for any extra work you take on. (For more on office housework, flip to the next chapter.)

If you can't run experiments within the constraints of your job, look outside the company. "Join industry groups, go to conferences, volunteer for a nonprofit," advises Dillon. This doesn't have to mean additional time away from your family. Consider involving your kids in any volunteer work you take on, for example, or see if there are virtual events that you can attend during a lunch break.

The third way to test your hypotheses is to have conversations. Find people who are doing what you think you want to do and ask them lots of questions. Ideally these will be folks whose involvement with their family and community is similar to yours, so they can reflect on how possible it is to do the job you aspire to and meet your family commitments. Listen carefully and critically, so that you don't just hear what you want to hear.

Form a personal board of directors

Don't go it alone. Work with others to kick the tires on your hypotheses and share the results of your experiments. Invite four or five people to serve as your informal board of directors, making sure to include a few fellow working mothers who understand the realities of your life. You might tell them, "I'm doing some exploring about what I want from work and I'd love to talk with you on occasion to get your feedback on my direction." Include any mentors and trusted professional peers. And if your manager is receptive include them as well. "Not all bosses may be supportive," says Dillon, "but if you have a manager who you can bounce career ideas off of, take advantage of that."

Don't be afraid to dig deep into your past, Dillon says: "I have people who I haven't talked with in years who call me when they're considering a job change or a career transition." Check in with this board of directors on a regular basis to update them on your thinking and ask for input.

Think long term

This work shouldn't just be in service of getting your next job. "Career design is different than a job-search strategy," says Koloc, and the question you should be asking yourself, he advises, is not "What job do I want?" but "What life do I want?" Think about where you want to be in 5, 10, 20 years. Consider what type of relationship you'd like to have with your family as your children grow up. Talk to colleagues and friends who have children who are older than yours to help you anticipate what types of challenges you may face as a parent later on in your career. Of course, you have to answer more immediate questions about what you want in your current job or your next, but do so only in the context of your longer, larger career goals.

When you're already deep into a career

Mid-career professionals can and do make big changes—even those with rent and college tuition to pay. "Your ability to turn the ship is no different, but the speed at which you turn it is going to be slower," says Koloc. "If you're 35 and have two kids, it's going to take longer to explore." There's good news though, he says. "You have more clues as to what you want and enjoy." The important thing is to not feel stuck. "You may feel locked into a job, a higher salary, a higher title because you have more responsibilities, like a mortgage and kids, and sure, you may need to take fewer risks, but you don't want to settle for a job or career you're not happy with," says Dillon.

Buckle down on your finances

One of the main reasons people give for staying in a job or career they don't love is money. "Take steps to give yourself a financial cushion and a little psychological freedom," says Dillon. Make a budget if you don't have one. Look for ways to lower the amount of money you need each month: downsize your house, move to one car, and drop unnecessary expenses. Involve your family in this effort, making sure everyone in your household is on the same page about reducing spending and the reason behind it. It's not always easy to convince your family to rein in expenses, but having a financial buffer will make it more likely that when you find something meaningful, you'll be able to act on it.

Make the time

"I have yet to meet anybody who wouldn't benefit from setting aside dedicated time to sit down and think about what they want from work," says Koloc. Schedule a time in your calendar to reflect on your career. While it can be difficult to find time in an already full schedule, even if it's just an hour every other week, you're going to make some progress. If you have older kids, you might even involve them in the process, asking them to also reflect on what a meaningful career will look like for them in the future. "Sometimes just thinking about it will get the ball rolling, and then, often, the change becomes inevitable," says Koloc.

Case Study: Get Your Finances in Order

Tim Groves liked his job at a civil litigation law firm. But he didn't love it. "I didn't get up in the morning excited to go to work," he says. "And I knew if I continued on that career path, it wasn't going to get better either." Making a career change wasn't straightforward though, given that he didn't want to jeopardize his ability to provide for his family while searching for another role. He was interested in mission-driven work, so he started by talking to people in the nonprofit world and signed up for automated job listings. "I volunteered and served on boards, and I had friends and relatives who worked in nonprofits so I had an inkling of what I could do with a law degree in a nonprofit setting," he says.

He also did a few informational interviews with people he respected who had made similar transitions. He was careful in how he set up these conversations. "I told people that I wasn't miserable at my current job, but that I was looking around and would love their perspective," he explains. "I also mentioned that I had a mortgage and a family so didn't want to broadcast this."

To broaden his network, he became more active in his volunteer and board work and upped the pro bono law work he was doing. "I put myself in contact with people who could connect me to an opportunity or who could vouch for me when one came up."

Tim and his wife had supported each other through several career transitions, but this time, as he says, "the stakes were higher because we had kids, school tuitions, and college looming on the horizon." Given that Tim was going to almost certainly take a pay cut, he and his wife came up with a budget and the lowest salary figure he could take. To give themselves more financial flexibility, they downsized and moved from a one-family to a two-family house where rent from tenants could help pay the mortgage.

About a year and a half after starting the process, Tim took a job as a development officer at the Rhode Island Foundation. "The process wasn't always easy, but I feel good about where I ended up," he says.

Adapted from content posted on hbr.org, February 4, 2015 (product #H01V4K).

"Office Housework" Gets in Women's Way

by Deborah M. Kolb and Jessica L. Porter

Quick Takes

All too often, women are tasked with invisible work in organizations—taking notes, planning events, and so on—that take precious time but don't lead to promotion. To break the trend:

- Turn requests into opportunities for growth

- Calculate the time and cost of your participation

- Demonstrate the work's value, and use it to expand your role

- Suggest taking turns—and remind others when the time comes

More often than not, women are the ones who help others when asked—they plan the meetings, take the notes, and take on other types of "office housework," in Rosabeth Moss Kanter's immortal phrase. These thankless-but-necessary tasks keep organizations humming. But as Facebook COO Sheryl Sandberg and Wharton professor Adam Grant noted in a *New York Times* article, while women are expected to do more of this work, they don't get credit for it and suffer backlash when they refuse to do it. "When a woman declines to help a colleague, people like her less and her career suffers," they wrote, citing different studies by professors Madeline Heilman, Joan C. Williams, and Joyce K. Fletcher. "But when a man says no, he faces no backlash. A man who doesn't help is 'busy'; a woman is 'selfish.'"[1]

Office "housework" is often invisible, so its value to a team is underappreciated. That fact creates one of the hidden barriers that can keep women from ascending to more senior leadership roles. In our decades studying this phenomenon, we've found four negotiation strategies that work.

15 Office Housework Tasks to Watch Out For

by Joan C. Williams and Marina Multhaup

- Taking the notes
- Procuring the conference room
- Getting everyone on the conference line
- Planning parties
- Buying the gifts for birthdays, retirements, baby showers, and so on
- Ordering lunch
- Organizing lower-level employees
- Mentoring activities
- Serving on committees that are not linked to revenue or core business goals
- Handling less-valued clients
- Handling HR tasks
- Handling routine work vs. work that is central to business strategy
- Organizing off-site events
- Keeping the task list
- Keeping the trains running vs. strategy and big-picture thinking

Adapted from "For Women and Minorities to Get Ahead, Managers Must Assign Work Fairly," on hbr.org, March 5, 2018 (product #H04774).

- **Turn a request for help into a negotiation.** Alexandra, a project manager, was asked by her boss to support a leader who has having family issues and needed help doing his work. Her boss asked her to be an "acting director." Alexandra negotiated this request into a promotion: She agreed to help, provided she would be named to a "director" role after the helping period ended and the leader returned to his job.

- **Ascertain the cost of your contribution.** Helping is not a free good. Not only does it take time away from your day job, but it can exact a toll on your health and family. When Patria, a program leader in an NGO, was asked by her director to help a colleague whose team was having trouble managing its workload, she agreed. But when she factored in the additional time required to help her colleague, her prorated hourly pay dropped dramatically. When she pointed this out to the director in stark dollar terms, Patria was able to negotiate for more resources in order to continue to help without putting in more time.

- **Demonstrate the value of your help.** In our work, we have seen how women successfully incorporate their helping work into an expanded version of their jobs by showing the value of the work. That is

what Isobel, a communications manager, did. After
initially helping another division with a government client and saving an important relationship,
the other division kept asking for her "fixing" help.
Although she liked being seen as a fixer, she knew
she could not continue and still keep up with her
job. By showing the value of her work to the other
division, she negotiated the fixing work she was
doing into a new expanded role, with a commen-
surate title and raise.

- **If the ask is more personal than professional, build
in reciprocity.** In the examples above, helping
benefited the organization. But getting the coffee
and planning the office party are more personal.
When negotiating these types of requests, ask for
reciprocity—if I do this, then what will you do?
Allison, a senior leader, was always willing to take
her turn getting the coffee—with the proviso, "I'll
do it today and next time it will be your turn." And
she made sure the other person remembered.

Negotiating the conditions of your help is good for you
as an individual and good for your organization. When
you help without conditions, you train people to expect
that you will continue to do so. But when you negotiate
the conditions of your help, it can be a small win for you.
As we have found in our work, these small wins can start

to accumulate into bigger gains. Sandberg and Grant note it doesn't have to be the case that "no good deed goes unpunished." But reversing that behavior requires women to place value on their help and to negotiate to have that work acknowledged and rewarded.

Adapted from content posted on hbr.org, April 16, 2015 (product #H020J5).

Questions for Navigating the Second Half of Your Career

by Palena Neale

Quick Takes

- Reflect on what you want or are missing in your career
- Give yourself permission to change
- Make a list of champions, mentors, and others who can help you
- Identify and learn new skills to meet your new goals

For many women in their 50s, the combination of newly empty nests, extensive professional experience, and financial freedom make it the perfect time to finally accelerate their careers. But that's often easier said than done. Women often have to counter their own limiting beliefs, as well as society's expectations, about what this time of life can mean—accelerating your career versus retirement fantasies of slippers and golf. Practically speaking, this means carving out time to reflect, plan, challenge, experiment, and do.

As a 50-something woman, what can you do today to reenergize your career and make the most of this next phase of your life? Here are four questions that I've found can help anyone rethink and achieve their professional goals:

1. What would your career look like if nothing was in your way?

Your 50s are the time to invest in the second half of your life. Find a quiet, reflective moment to ask yourself:

- What's missing in your life? In your work?

- What kind of difference do you want to make?

- What does your dream job look like?

- What career move would you make if you knew you couldn't fail?

- What do you want to be remembered for?

Some of my clients dream about advancing into more-senior leadership positions; some envision crafting a new, more fulfilling role for themselves; while others have considered leaving their organizations entirely to become entrepreneurs or focus on personal projects.

For example, Isabelle (names have been changed), a senior technical lead in a regional office, enjoyed an impressive career, with several published books and key industry reference pieces. At 52, she had just sent her son off to college, and she came to coaching for advice on how to make the most of her next 10 years. She recognized that she "had more time, energy, focus, and freedom to reinvest in [her] work life," and she wanted to push herself out of her "narrow technical comfort zone" and focus on leading others.

With her son out of the house, she was no longer limited to local opportunities, so she started applying for jobs globally. In less than six months, Isabelle landed a leadership position in another country.

Another client, Florence, was a senior manager in a multinational organization who came to coaching to talk about a troubling trend she'd been experiencing: less competent, less experienced men kept moving past her into leadership positions for which she felt more than qualified. She was deeply committed to her organization and believed that by taking up a leadership position, she would be better poised to effect change both directly and by influencing others. She began actively promoting herself and applying for leadership positions within her organization, and after 14 months, she was asked to lead a major department.

2. What permissions do you need to give yourself in order to become who you want to be?

Many women get stuck in some version of the authenticity trap: They hold on to too-rigid definitions of a singular self that don't permit them to engage with and develop other potential identities (for example, a leader) or skills (for instance, networking).

Isabelle never allowed herself to ask for help, feeling that it would run counter to her core values of independence, autonomy, and strength. Florence prided herself in being someone who put her head down and got the work done, not someone who sought the spotlight. By interrogating these limiting beliefs and exploring how they created unnecessary professional roadblocks, each woman was able to expand her identity and enrich her skill set.

Isabelle started to appreciate asking for help as an important component of good leadership, rather than an indication of a lack of independence. Instead of attempting to find a new job entirely on her own, she reached out to her boss, who turned out to be a supportive ally and actually introduced Isabelle to the hiring manager at her new organization.

Similarly, when Florence reframed her negative assumptions about self-promotion, she was able to find ways to promote herself that aligned with both her goals of increased visibility within the company and her values of humility. After becoming more open to being in the spotlight, she enlisted her boss's support to present her team's work at a senior management retreat, joined a high-level working group, and presented her research at an international conference.

3. How can you build and access your support network?

At first, neither Isabelle nor Florence leveraged their networks to further their ambitions, so I urged them both to conduct a relationship audit. The process is simple: Open a Word or Excel file (or grab a pen and paper), and write down as many names as you can for each category:

1. Career champions: Who will sing my praises?

2. Sources of feedback: Who will give me honest feedback on my performance and challenge me to develop?

3. Emotional support system: Who will give me a positive boost?

4. Organizational sages: Who will help me understand the ins and outs of the organization?

5. Mentors: Who will help me think through personal and professional decisions?

6. Connectors: Who has a large and diverse network and is willing to introduce me to others?

7. Power people: Who has the power to make things happen?

After completing this audit, Florence reached out to colleagues who helped her identify new opportunities and connect with key decision makers. Similarly, this exercise helped Isabelle leverage existing relationships to connect with important people both inside and outside her organization, ultimately leading to her new role.

The exercise was valuable not only because it helped both women to identify useful contacts, but also because it allowed them to see how they themselves routinely supported others in their organizations. This enabled them to reframe networking as a shared, reciprocal activity rather than a purely transactional pursuit, making them feel more comfortable and confident with the process.

4. What do you need to learn?

Good leaders are constantly learning. What skills, information, or self-knowledge do you need to get to where you want to be?

For example, both Isabelle and Florence found that they had to upskill in order to meet their late-career goals. Updating CVs, preparing bios and LinkedIn profiles, and engaging on social media were all skills they needed to refine and/or learn from scratch. Not only did they gain valuable technical skills through this process, but the exercise also helped both women refamiliarize themselves with their professional accomplishments, building confidence and improving their ability to self-promote.

While I've focused on helping women who are looking to ramp up their careers in their 50s, this advice can apply to anyone. If you are a few decades into your career and looking to accelerate, think about what you want to be, do, and feel; recognize the beliefs and assumptions that might be standing in your way; and identify what new knowledge or skills will help you reach your goal. And when you inventory your supporters, don't forget to include yourself. You are your own strongest ally—so move forward boldly, and with no regrets.

Adapted from "4 Questions to Help Women Navigate the Second Half of Their Careers," on hbr.org, September 9, 2020 (product #H05UFF).

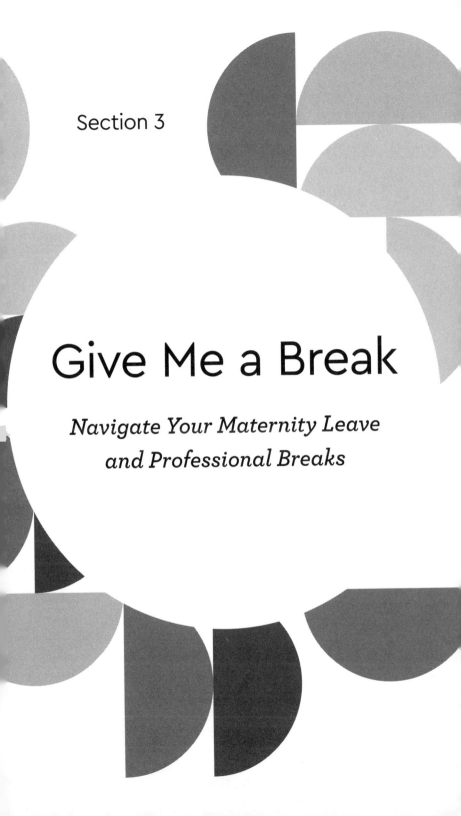

Section 3

Give Me a Break

*Navigate Your Maternity Leave
and Professional Breaks*

Planning Maternity or Family Leave: A Guide

by Rebecca Knight

Quick Takes

- Find out how much time you're entitled to
- Draft a transition-out plan and transition-back memo
- Set communication boundaries for your leave
- Let go of work projects while you're away
- Check in with your boss before your return

Taking any amount of time off work can be nerve-wracking, even if it's for a happy event like having or adopting a baby. What's the best way to get ready for your maternity or family leave? How should you set boundaries? Should you check in with your team while you're out? And how do you plan your return?

What the Experts Say

Very few organizations have "a standard operating procedure" for employees taking parental time off, says Joan C. Williams, founding director of the Center for WorkLife Law at the University of California's Hastings College of the Law. All too often, they "Band-Aid together a solution every time someone needs to go on leave," letting the burden fall on the parent-to-be. The lack of parental leave plans in most U.S. organizations "reflects the disconnect between people's personal lives and their work lives," says Lotte Bailyn, professor emerita at the MIT Sloan School of Management. "It should be easier than it is," she says. "The fact is that people have babies; they go on

National Guard leave; they get sick; and their parents get sick"—in other words, the need for leave is an inevitable fact of employment. The key is to assume a positive outlook. "It's best if you assume it's going to go well." Here are some pointers.

Get a head start

You want to start thinking about how you will manage your leave—how much time you will take, whether you'll be in contact, how you will transition back—well in advance. So before you go on leave, investigate your organization's policies surrounding how much leave you're entitled to. This information, depending on the size of your organization, is usually available online or in an employee handbook. If you're unsure, contact your HR department. But be mindful about timing. "When you talk to HR depends on your organization's culture," says Bailyn. She says that some people worry that they will be "written off" once they announce their family plans. "Don't wait until the last minute," though. There is a considerable amount of paperwork and contingency planning that needs to happen, and "it takes time for other people to figure out" how to manage your absence, Bailyn says.

How to Negotiate Maternity Leave

by Amy Gallo

To get the leave you want, understand your company's policy and appropriately advocate for your needs. Follow these steps to guide your negotiation.

1. **Know what you're entitled to.** Review your organization's employee manual or talk with someone in HR to see what policies are already in place. It can be helpful to know what benefits you're guaranteed by the government as well.

2. **Ask yourself if that's enough.** Will it meet my needs? Will I have enough time off? Will the pay be sufficient? Talk with your partner or spouse, too.

3. **Explore alternatives.** Ask around and find out what precedents colleagues have set with their parental leaves and what companies comparable to your own offer their employees.

4. **Start with your manager.** Bring up the topic with your boss first so that you can problem-solve together and come up with a plan.

5. **Accept that negotiating won't always help.** If the company is in financial stress, you don't have a great relationship with your boss, or your performance has been suffering, it might not be a good time to ask for more.

Adapted from "How to Negotiate Your Parental Leave," on hbr.org, October 25, 2012 (product #H009LK).

Devise a transition strategy

If possible, about a month before your leave, ask your supervisor for help in creating a "transition-out plan," says Williams. This memo "defines everything you do" for the organization, describes where each of your projects stands, and identifies the specific colleagues or temporary workers who will "fill in for you during your leave," she says. Without a plan like this, warns Williams, "your work will be abruptly dumped on others." Bailyn recommends involving your colleagues. "You need to work collectively and creatively to figure out how the work will get done [in your absence]," she says. This should motivate others. "Team members will realize that if and when they need something, the group will support them, too."

Plan your return

In addition to the transition-out plan, you should create a "transition-back memo" to help set expectations and ensure an "appropriate flow" of work for your return, Williams says. "It's very common to come back from leave with either no work or an overwhelming amount of work—both of these are undesirable and a recipe for high attrition." Also think about how you'd like to structure your return to the office. "Be realistic about whether you want to do a gradual return to work"—where you start out as part-time and work up to full-time—whether you'd like to negotiate to work from home one day or week, "or if you'd like to be permanent part-time," she says. Then, depending on your relationship with your boss, explore those possibilities before you go on leave. "If it's going to freak out your manager if you bring this up beforehand, don't," says Williams. "But if your manager is more chill, why not have the information?"

Establish boundaries

While it's "illegal for a company to ask you to work on your leave," says Williams, "it's practical and considerate to let your colleagues know that you're reachable." She suggests saying something like: *If you need a crucial piece of information from me, here's how to get in touch, and I'll do my best to get back to you as soon as I can.* Just knowing that you're there "if something important comes up will make everyone more comfortable," says Bailyn. And if your leave is longer than three months, you might also consider having regular, planned meetings with your team "either in-person or by videoconference" at the three-, four-, and five-month mark, she says. "These meetings are a way to check in with your group and find how everything's going," which will help you when you return.

Let go . . .

Don't be tempted to keep tabs on work projects and office politics while you're away. "You can't say, 'While I am out, I want to be involved in A, B, and C.' You need to let go," says Williams. Failing to do so will likely lead to frustration. "You'll be torn between your very intense new responsibilities and very intense old responsibilities," she says. Involving yourself with work projects while you're on leave is also unfair to the colleagues filling in for you, says Bailyn. "Think about [your leave] as an opportunity to help other people develop," she says. After all, "you should have defined and planned how projects will be dealt with [in your absence]," she says. "Have confidence that your people will handle things the way you would want them to be handled."

. . . Then gear up

About two weeks before your leave is over, Williams recommends calling your boss to set up a one-hour meeting to review your transition-back plan. "You're not legally obligated to do this—it's a judgment call—but if it were me, I'd do it," she says. The alternative to this preemptive meeting is waiting to discuss your return on your first day back, which increases the likelihood you will "have either no work or too much work," she says. It's smart to

Practice Runs

For mothers who have just had a child, returning from maternity leave often involves executing on a new set of complicated logistics. Daisy Dowling, founder and CEO of Workparent, advises "trying to get ahead of them" as much as possible to "minimize the sting."

Start with the basics: The first day you go back to work shouldn't be the first day your baby goes to daycare or stays home with a new nanny. Dowling recommends doing at least a few practice drop-offs or asking your sitter to start a week early. "Get your child used to the process and accustomed to the caregiver," she says. Dry runs will help you, too. "Get up in the morning, take a shower, put on your work clothes, feed the baby, take her to daycare, get your Starbucks, and drive to the office," she says. "Then literally turn right back around." If you're nursing, try to add a pumping session or two in there as well.

check in with your team too before your official return, says Bailyn.

Strategically plan and communicate the day you'll return, as well. Experts recommend working two or three days in your first week back on the job. Starting mid-week—on a Wednesday or Thursday—allows you to ease back in and ensures that you don't have a five-day stretch of work from the start.

Be honest with yourself

This prereturn check-in is also the time when you'll likely make final arrangements about your transition. Remember, though, it's a fluid situation. "You don't know [in advance] how you'll feel physically and emotionally [about going back to work] so you can't make hard and fast decisions [ahead of time]," says Bailyn. If you are having second thoughts about going back full-time, think creatively about how you could make the situation work. Bailyn recommends bringing your team in on these discussions. "The problem with flexible arrangements is that they are often individually negotiated and kept in secret," she says. A better option is to work out a proposed plan with your team that delineates "how the work would get done" if you went part-time and then "bring it to your manager," she says. "It could be in the spirit of, 'Let's try this for two months and see if it works.'"

Case Study: Work with Your Team on a Workload Plan

Erin Quinn-Kong, the editor in chief of *Austin Monthly*, found out she was pregnant only a couple of days before her company's new publisher started on the job. She decided to hold off sharing her news until she was 16 weeks pregnant.

"I had been here five years, but I had a brand-new boss—I wanted to establish a relationship with him before I told him I was pregnant," said Erin.

By the time she told her publisher, Erin had already mapped out a plan for how she would structure her leave and also provided suggestions for how her staff could do the work while she was away. She also talked to her team. "We discussed potentially bringing in someone new at the bottom, but the other editors here decided they wanted to handle it themselves," she said. "We planned as far in advance as possible, and we were all working hard now to get ahead."

During her leave—which consisted of eight weeks' disability pay and an additional four weeks of both paid and unpaid time off—Erin said she went "dark" but was reachable to her staff in the event that something important came up. "I trusted them. I knew they were good at their jobs, and they were not going to call me for 'in the weeds' type stuff. They would figure it out. It would be a good learning experience for them."

It has also been a good learning experience for Erin. "I've gotten better at delegating since I announced I was pregnant," she said.

When her maternity leave was over, Erin returned to her job full-time but worked from home on Wednesdays—an arrangement she had already worked out with her publisher. (She started this flex-time arrangement at the beginning of her third trimester, which "really helped with the transition.")

Her daughter was in daycare, one block away from Erin's house. "I do drop-off, and my husband does pickup," she said. "That's the plan."

Adapted from "Planning Maternity or Paternity Leave: A Professional's Guide," on hbr.org, May 29, 2015 (product #H0241F) and "How to Return to Work After Taking Parental Leave," on hbr.org, August 2, 2019 (product #H052W1).

What You Need to Know About Pumping During Work Travel

by Julia Beck

Quick Takes

- Identify any relevant policies your company has in place

- Ask your boss or organization for what you need

- Create a grassroots support group to share information

- Reach out to friends for advice when planning your trip

- Arrive early for flights, so you have time to pump

- Contact your hotel in advance to secure needed supplies

Any new mom who is returning to work is coping with a challenging professional and personal transition. Regardless of how well the employee has planned for their return, the reality of it is startling. And if that return involves business travel, and that mother has chosen to nurse, it's even more complicated. They need to quickly become an expert on the necessities and nuances of pumping on the road.

While it's common for new parents to feel stressed about juggling life at work and home, for a pumping, traveling mother, the stress can be heightened. "Finding the time and the space to pump [while traveling for work] made me feel like I had something to prove in terms of still being competent and a high achiever in the workplace," explains Lindsey, a pharma rep. "I felt as though I had to show that I was 'still me.'" This pressure affected both her milk supply and her self-esteem.

Nyla Beth, a principal in a large government consulting firm, also felt intense pressure to get back on the road quickly after having her first baby, though she said it got easier after baby number two, when she also had a more senior position in the organization. "I had a clearer voice, more experience, increased confidence, and the ability to chart my own path. While my higher level of seniority certainly created new pressures, it also left me much more in charge of myself."

Ask, Advocate, and Organize

One stumbling block is that company policies and benefits aren't clear—either to employees or to their managers. Employees have no choice but to ask and advocate for themselves, even if the timing feels awkward or they're not sure how the company will respond. For example, Lindsey came back to work after giving birth to her first child just after the company had gone through a round of layoffs. Given the corporate climate, she felt enormous pressure to attend the company's annual sales meeting, which meant leaving her 14-week-old son at home. "I went about looking for how to pump and travel," she told me. "I came across Milk Stork, a milk shipment service, and took it to my manager. She was somewhat supportive in that she took it to HR, but at the same time it felt less than genuine, as she kept telling me how well formula worked for her." In the end, her manager shared that the firm *already offered* Milk Stork. Lindsey was glad, but said, "I really did not understand why this was not communicated to me in the first place." At least Lindsey's company had a policy—many firms still have ad hoc or muddled policies, if any.

Another tactic is grassroots organization. Nyla Beth decided to tackle the lack of official information in her organization by creating an ad hoc mentorship program so that new parents could find each other and share insights. Other parents I've talked to have also used this grassroots approach. For example, Marisa, a former senior executive at Discovery Communications and mother of three, compiled a "how to travel" file of information that she shared with pumping employees before they took their first business trips. It included everything from airport hacks to equipment strategy. Marisa made a point of celebrating an employee's return to work and serving as the maternal go-to, filling in the gaps at her company.

Become a Travel-Logistics Master

Pumping, storing, and transporting milk while juggling client needs, unfamiliar office buildings, and airplane schedules is one of the toughest logistical challenges a new parent can master.

One of the biggest hurdles of pumping on the road is the tactical management of the milk itself—how to preserve it and how to get it home. This is a major point of anxiety for pumping employees who work incredibly hard—transporting equipment, securing private spaces, finding appropriate times, and so on. It is complicated to say the least. Losing milk (aka liquid gold) is a devastating blow after so much planning and work, but it's not uncommon at airports. Airports and airport security checkpoints vary in terms of their knowledge and ability to get parents carrying milk through to the gate.

In the United States, legislation was passed under President Obama that called for a universal process and procedure at TSA checkpoints for breast milk, baby formula, and similar items.[1] While the law is on the books, it is neither widely understood nor consistently enforced. Kate Torgersen, the mother of three who started Milk Stork, explains that for parents who prefer to carry their milk rather than ship it, the company includes a printed card with information on the TSA's policies to carry and show to skeptical TSA agents. The parents I talked to offered some other hard-won tips:

- Be early to everything. Show up earlier to the airport than you're used to, so you can pump before you take off, and reserve early check-ins at your hotels to facilitate pumping on arrival.

- Tell a flight attendant what you are doing when pumping on a flight—they can advocate for you and clarify or cover for long restroom usage.

- Make it easier on yourself by choosing appropriate nursing clothing and undergarments. Easy-access clothing lines such as Loyal Hana offer professional clothes with user-friendly hidden zippers, for instance. Belabumbum and Bravado Designs make comfortable yet supportive nursing bras perfect for business travel.

- Ask friends or Facebook groups for the best airports for nursing to help you plan your layovers. (In my discussions with working mothers, Los Angeles International Airport came up again and again.) Research pumping locations in airport terminals in advance—Mamava offers an app with information on different airports.

- Call your hotel in advance and ask about refrigeration options. Do not use the minibar—the temperature is not cold enough, and chances are you will be billed for anything you remove to make room for your milk.

- Invest in wipes and other ways to keep your equipment sterile and clean on the go, and plan to maximize bags, as well as bottles, for pumped milk. They will take up less space and travel better.

- Consider an all-in-one pump such as the Willow to fit in your bra directly. A manual pump, too, is an inexpensive addition to your travel accessories. This "just in case" item requires no batteries and will resolve issues of full breasts quickly without power.

- Use the United States Breastfeeding Committee web page as a resource on traveling and breastfeeding, which includes details on the newly passed Friendly Airports for Mothers Improvement Act.

The logistics around pumping as a working mother are hard enough, even before travel is added to the mix. Do your homework and make a plan to ensure that your business trip goes as smoothly as possible.

Adapted from "What Nursing Parents Need to Know About Pumping During Work Travel," on hbr.org, June 14, 2017 (product #H03PQM).

How to Transition into a Professional Break

by Daisy Dowling

Quick Takes

- Have a clear plan for how long you'll take off
- Explain your exit clearly and professionally
- Be prepared for pushback or negative comments
- Stay in contact with folks in your professional network
- Volunteer and consult while you're away

You've decided to take time away from work, to put your focus on responsibilities at home for a while or to get some concentrated time with your kids. But the raft of emotions attached to a professional exit can swell to very large proportions. You may feel guilty, excited, conflicted, angry, relieved, and many other emotions in between—perhaps all at the same time.

You may have also heard professional horror stories about women (and men) who have taken breaks and were never able to find their way back into the professional world, or who did, but in reduced roles and at just a fraction of their previous salaries. Or you've heard breaks discussed in a strange, engineering-esque vocabulary: "off-ramp," "on-ramp," career "architecture," or "design," and so forth.

Unfortunately for working parents, there's no off-boarding playbook. But there are strategies that can help—specific techniques that can make your transition as effective and nonstressful as possible. I call this *career-break preventative care*, maneuvers that will let you take a true and complete career break with minimal hurt or headache, while also setting you up to enhance your network or career for your return.

Step Away from the Hype

While it's usually true that it's easier to find a job if you're already in one, and that taking a longer break does carry some real risks, it hardly spells the end of your modern-day professional ambitions. In today's world, moves in and out of the workforce are becoming both more frequent and more visible, and they're much more readily accepted now than they were even 10 years ago. Besides, you're not managing to statistics, or to the careers of *all* professionals, everywhere. You only have to make one career work—yours—and there's no reason you can't swing this as long you take an eyes-wide-open approach and the correct up-front actions.

Have an Endgame in Mind

Before you even start the transition out of the workforce, make sure you have a clear time frame in mind for how long you'll be out, so you can plan your way back in. If your goal is to return to work "later," it's all too easy to let one year off become 2, 2 become 5 . . . and then 10. On the other hand, if your goal is "to take 18 months at home and return to work when my youngest is in school full-time," you've got a goal to work toward. You'll be able to enjoy that first full year without worry or guilt, and you'll know to start interviewing around months 12 to 14.

Leave Your Organization Well

One of the easiest ways to ultimately get back into the workforce is to return to your past employer. No matter how unpalatable that option looks right now, it's best to keep it open. Even if you're leaving because you feel you've been mistreated in some way, don't be brutally negative in your exit interview, throw a snit, or throw your manager under the bus when asked why you're leaving. As in any relationship, how you break up is how you'll be remembered.

Say it plain—without an edge

"Mary, this may or may not come as a surprise, but after careful consideration I've decided that for the next few years, I need to focus my full attentions and talents on my family." Like a good newspaper article, the most important information should be conveyed up front, factually, and neutrally. Don't wait five minutes into the conversation to make your announcement, and don't address any gripes you had about the lifestyle or hours on the job when breaking the news—those are in the rearview mirror.

Be a class act—regardless of your feelings

Even if your manager screamed at you about missing a weekly update meeting to take your sick child to the pediatrician, it's time to rise above. Remember: Last impressions are lasting impressions, and yours need to convey your value and style as a professional. Saying "I've appreciated the four years I spent here, and the opportunity to be part of a great team" puts you in a much better long-term position than a negative statement will.

Play through the negative reaction

Your manager may be surprised, or even angry. Maybe you were the "work-life poster child" the company wanted to keep, or maybe your departure means the department loses head count. Be prepared for negative reactions—pushback, derision, irritation, disbelief—and rehearse the jujitsu moves you can make to neutralize them. Empathize and acknowledge: "I understand if this is a surprise." Make things more personal: "I understand your point of view as a leader of the company, but I've made this decision as an individual, and a parent." And praise: "My decision has nothing to do with how I see you as a manager. You've been a great advocate for me, and I appreciate it."

Keep an open mind

Many of my working-parent coachees are shocked, upon resigning, to find out how much their organizations value them—and are suddenly willing to provide new roles, more flexibility, even sabbatical leaves in a desperate bid to keep them. As firm as your intention to leave is, remain open to new options that are offered. You may find an unexpected solution that's actually better than the one you've committed to. At the very least, it's worth a conversation.

Put on blinders

Inevitably, any working parent leaving his or her job for anything remotely to do with family reasons will be on the receiving end of editorial comments—lots and lots of them, some clumsy ("Couldn't take it, huh?") to well intentioned but disheartening ("Be careful—my law school roommate left after her first was born and she could never find a job again"). The comments have nothing to do with you, so ignore them. Put on blinders, look down the straightaway, and run your own race, with the guardrails and mile markers you've set for yourself, not the ones others set for you.

Become a consultant

Once the announcement has been made, go above and beyond to help your colleagues transition into their future without you. Summaries, checklists, training the person who picks up your work—your job is to help the organization manage without you. Stay late a few days to demonstrate how committed you are to supporting colleagues through your departure. You'll look like the top-flight professional you are—efficient, professional, and graceful to boot.

Actively Plan Your Return

You may feel tempted to put any thought of your career on hold while you're taking time with your family or responsibilities at home. But positioning yourself for success when you return takes careful planning throughout your time off.

Take your relationships with you

Keep your professional connections—with managers, colleagues, mentors, mentees, and everyone in between—intact and communicate how valuable those people are to you. Statements like "While we won't be working together anymore, I want you to know that I've always considered you a mentor and will continue to" or "I certainly hope we get to be members of the same team again" appeal to and leave lasting positive impressions with the crustiest of colleagues. Think of your professional network as a portfolio, and make sure that no important assets fall out of it as you change roles.

Additionally, have at least one touch point with the people you used to work with at least once every quarter. That may be lunch, a visit to the workplace, or as small as a text message or social media touchpoint. You may even offer to do some part-time consulting work—helping out during a busy season, for example—as a means of keeping the lines of communication open, your skills sharp, and your value on display. The point here is: *Never* let the relationships you worked so hard to establish go completely stale.

Have, and keep adding to, a "who can hire me" list

Whether or not your past organization is an option, what about the place you worked for before that? What about your past clients or suppliers? Could they bring you on board? Or old colleagues who've moved on to successful careers elsewhere? Or the other parents at your kids' school, who also work in your field? When you do start looking for a new role, you want to have an immediate call list of 10 to 15 viable options.

Keep your résumé fresh by volunteering—strategically

It's fine to take on the task of organizing the annual bake sale at your kids' school, but a prospective employer is unlikely to be impressed by this activity unless you happen to be interviewing at a bakery. That advice may come across as harsh, but this is your time we're talking about, and your time has value; you want to spend it wisely and know what the investment will yield you. On the other hand, serving in a leadership role with a trade group, taking an adjunct teaching position in your field, writing for an industry publication, or doing pro bono consulting for a few relevant startups or nonprofits or other similar work all speaks well to your professional capabilities and can-do.

Be able to explain your *why*, and why now

You're going to be asked to explain both your career break and your desire to return to work, most likely by an interviewer with little interest in your life story. Be able to explain both in two sentences or less, and in an honest, confident way. It's helpful to interview or rehearse interviewing well before you go back to work, so you seem as crisp, convincing, and on message as possible.

Anyone making the transition out of the workforce will inevitably have some concerns and self-doubt. But by focusing on career-break preventative care, you can make the transition resound to your credit and keep doors open for the future.

Adapted from "When You're Leaving Your Job Because of Your Kids," on hbr .org, April 11, 2017 (product #H03LD7) and Workparent: The Complete Guide to Succeeding on the Job, Staying True to Yourself, and Raising Happy Kids, *by Daisy Dowling, Harvard Business Review Press, 2021.*

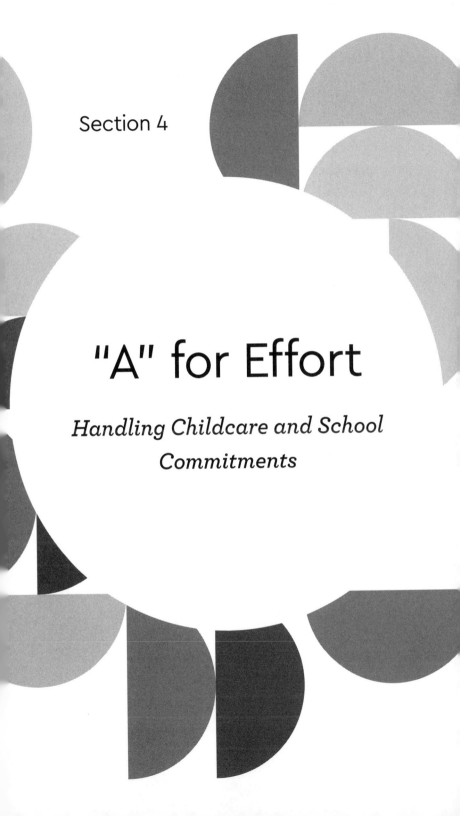

Section 4

"A" for Effort

Handling Childcare and School Commitments

11

Making a Plan for Childcare—and Uncertainties

by Avni Patel Thompson

Quick Takes

- List your top three priorities
- Create a plan A, B, C . . . and Q
- Share your plans with your support team
- Have weekly look-ahead meetings with your partner
- Talk through backup plans for the trickiest parts

isa and Geoff are a dual-career couple, living in Chicago with their 6- and 8-year-old sons. Until the spring of 2020, managing two careers and two kids was challenging—especially without family in town—but they had figured out a routine that worked for them. The boys were in kindergarten and second grade at a neighborhood school they loved that also had a great after-school program. Work was demanding and engaging but manageable. Like most families today, it wasn't easy, but it worked.

Then Covid-19 hit and the foundation of every working family's careful balance was pulled out from under them—namely, school and childcare. While Lisa and Geoff managed to cobble things together for the rest of the school year and through the summer, they held out hope that the fall would bring a return to some semblance of structure and certainty. That hope was shattered when, like many school districts across the country, their school announced options for 100% remote learning or a limited hybrid model of two days in school and three days remote.

The global pandemic certainly changed the way parents manage the work-family balance and required new decisions to be made under extreme stress and uncertainty, from whether to send a child back to an in-person classroom or daycare center to whether they can afford the cost of a part-time tutor, nanny, or sitter to whether now is the time to move closer to family for help. But even without a global pandemic, working mothers and fathers have to navigate uncertainty regularly. At a moment's notice, a child may become sick, a car can break down, or childcare can fall through.

As the founder and CEO of a company that builds software to help working parents manage the weekly complexities of running a family, I've seen variations of these dilemmas play out in thousands of households. We've found it's important to help parents build plans that work for their specific needs but that can also be adapted for a range of situations. Here are three steps for how you can do the same.

Start with Your Priorities

Parents are already master prioritizers, but in times of greater uncertainty, we need to protect the most important things—no matter what. Make a list of all possible priorities in your family's life. (To make it feel less daunting, focus on just the next quarter.) Then, pick the three that you want and need to protect most. This doesn't mean that the others aren't important, but just that anytime the top three are in jeopardy, the rest will have to take a back seat.

For instance, a single parent living close to high-risk grandparents may prioritize their extended family's health, their job, and their family's social and emotional health. A dual-working couple with elementary-aged kids may prioritize their relationship, consistent logistics, and both jobs. And a single-income family with a high-risk child may put education, physical health, and the parent's job first. Even though each of these families have core childcare needs, what their priorities are will guide the options they'll explore. A starter list of priorities for your consideration includes:

- Extended family

- Relationships with partner and kids

- Education and extra learning

- Physical health

- Social-emotional and mental health

- Socializing with friends

- Careers

- Financial health

Identify Options for Each Priority

Now that you have your top family priorities, consider how you'll best be able to maximize each, using three sets of options:

- **Plan A** is what is ideal, assuming all is going as planned.

- **Plan B** is your classic backup for when A falls through for the most obvious reasons, like a sick caregiver, an unexpected injury, a scheduling conflict, and so on.

- **Plan C** is your safety net, a potentially more drastic option if the first two stop being effective.

To create these plans, consider how options on the table might vary depending on your priorities. For instance, if extended family is a priority (as it was in the single parent example), your options may range from including grandparents within your bubble, choosing remote learning, or taking the opportunity to move closer to family. Protecting your career may mean reducing your childcare uncertainty by hiring a nanny to teaming up with two to three other families in a similar position and taking turns handling last-minute hiccups. (Chapter 14 tells you how to form such a parenting posse.) For education, you might decide to dedicate part of your budget for a private tutor who can supplement school curriculum, or you might keep learning opportunities at the forefront all week through real-world adventures and explorations. Consider your priorities and outline plans that work within them—what you want to do, a backup, and a third-tier option.

Put Plans in Action, with Ample Buffer

With the plans and options identified, it's time to enlist the help of others and create actionable weekly plans. Communicate the high-level points of your plan with people in your life—from your nanny or sitter to helpful neighbors and fellow parents in the community that you might be collaborating with.

With high-level plans in place, it's time to execute efficiently. We've found that the greater the uncertainty, the greater the gains in proactive planning versus last-minute reacting. Families we work with find that dedicating just 10 minutes to plan the week ahead results in fewer missed things, an ability to anticipate tricky spots, and a general feeling of family cohesion and collaboration. We also found that this approach saves roughly 20 minutes each day that is otherwise spent in researching, debating, and deciding—a number that easily adds up to a critical 10 hours a month.

To get started, schedule a standing weekly meeting with your partner (Sunday evening after the kids are in bed or first thing Saturday morning while your teens are sleeping in). Then, walk through six main areas:

1. Schedule review: Identify your meetings and high-priority items that you need dedicated time for and must work around.

2. Childcare shifts: Decide who handles pickup and drop-offs for school and daycare, or covers remote learning and childcare shifts throughout the week.

3. Meal plan: Jot down a quick list of lunches and dinners—nothing fancy—to save valuable time and energy during the week.

4. Key reminders: Talk through anything remaining that you need to remember.

5. Priority household to-dos: Pick no more than five chores to divvy up and add them to the schedule.

6. Backup planning: Talk about the trickiest parts of the week and how Plan B and Plan C will kick in if Plan A fails.

Despite the best-laid plans, we know each day can and will bring unexpected challenges. The goal, then, is not planned perfection, but something solid that you and your partner feel good about.

Families have never been under greater pressure to manage a tremendous amount of uncertainty, while needing to make critical decisions that involve our health, learning, and relationships. In this marathon, we need all the help we can get in lessening the uncertainty and creating plans that work for our specific needs, whether that's in the time of a worldwide pandemic or simply another week as working mothers.

Adapted from "How to Plan Child Care in Uncertain Times," on hbr.org, August 20, 2020 (product #H05TZ9).

12

How to Manage the Demands of School-Age Kids

by Daisy Dowling

Quick Takes

- Explain your reasons when you have to leave work
- Plan and bundle volunteer commitments
- Invest in the educational activities that matter most
- Try a "family study hall"
- Treat teachers as valued colleagues

Y our task list is endless; your stress level high. And a lot of the work and worry seems to be coming from one place: your child's school. From state testing, report cards, and parent-teacher conferences to end-of-year projects, summer childcare arrangements, and required health forms, it's a lot to handle. And that's *before* you start worrying whether your child might do better in math next year with a different teacher.

As a working parent, you've already got two jobs—and having two jobs isn't easy. But you're also going to spend a minimum of 13 years with a third critical role: stewarding your child's education. It's a position that comes with enormous hope and pressure. You want the absolute best for your children, and you're determined to oversee their school experience in a way that will set them up for success in college and life beyond. But it's a position that can create significant practical challenges for any family.

But here's the good news: There *are* effective ways to manage the overwhelming demands of drop-off, schoolwork, and parent-teacher meetings while still delivering and succeeding at work.

Here, gleaned from teachers, school administrators, and experienced parents themselves, are a few of the simple, specific techniques that put any working parent of school-age kids on their front foot—and they'll work for your family, too.

Explain the *why*, not just the *when*, of time away from work

Instead of telling your boss and colleagues that you'll be "out of the office tomorrow afternoon," explain that "I'll be leaving the office tomorrow afternoon for two hours for a meeting at Brandon's school. We've been concerned about his math scores, and we're talking with the teacher about how to support him over the summer and into next year. I'll be back online by 6 p.m., and we can go over the budget draft at tomorrow's meeting." The second statement makes it vastly easier for colleagues to understand, sympathize, and ally themselves with you—and does a better job of telegraphing your commitment to the job as well.

Plan and bundle volunteer commitments

Even with a very flexible job, it's unlikely that any working parent can make it to every bake sale, library fundraiser, and field trip. Here's what you do: In the first week of school, tell your child's teachers and/or the school's volunteer coordinators that you're eager to do your fair share, but that you will be doing it all in one go. You'll schedule a personal or vacation day well in advance and use it entirely for school volunteerism. Maybe you'll be the "reading helper" in your daughter's second-grade class in the morning, walk the school's neighborhood safety patrol in the afternoon, and take the minutes during the PTA fundraising committee meeting at 5 p.m. When the day is over, enjoy knowing that your yearly contribution has been made in full— and efficiently.

Invest your time where it matters most

All working parents have packed schedules, yet "in our desire to fully engage with our children's education, many of us gravitate to time-intensive activities that may not actually have much impact on their success in school," says Ariela Rozman, a leading K–12 education expert and founding partner of EdNavigator, a not-for-profit that provides custom coaching and tools for parents seeking to keep their children on track in school. Rozman adds: "There may be great reasons for you to take part in school fundraising, attend school events, or help your child with their homework each evening. Maybe you want to support the school community or simply to spend time together with your kid. But think about putting some time toward the things that are proven to produce great results too." Rozman cites "The Broken Compass: Parental

Involvement with Children's Education," a groundbreaking and comprehensive research study done by professors from the University of Texas and Duke University. They found a handful of habits that make a real difference, such as reading aloud to young kids and talking to teenagers about college plans.

Make "family study hall" a habit

Beat the nightly homework drama (the nagging, the power struggles, the bargaining, the tears) by setting a hard-and-fast time each evening that the whole family has study hall: silent, dedicated work time around the dining table. The kids do their homework and you catch up on office emails or reading. When the kitchen timer rings, study hall is over, and the whole family gets to enjoy downtime or a relaxing activity like watching a favorite TV program together. This routine may not be easy for the first few nights you try it, but the kids will quickly adjust, and the benefits are many. They will learn how to focus better, to work more efficiently, and to use the "sprint and recover" approach when tackling a large workload—all skills that will make them more successful and happier in school and in their futures. You'll also have established a clear boundary between work and play—something that's vital and healthy for the entire family in our always-on world.

Treat teachers and administrators as you would valued colleagues (because that's what they are)

For many parents, the parent-teacher relationship is fraught and unclear: Is the teacher an all-powerful evaluator, capable of changing your child's future with a few strokes of a red pen? Or a vendor who needs to be constantly nudged if you're going to get decent service? Will there be terrible consequences for your child if you dial into a parent-teacher meeting while on a business trip? The answer to all of those is no—but you *do* need to develop strong working relationships with the professionals teaching your child. To do so, think of a favorite coworker, one who you enjoy being staffed with on tough projects. The coworker is someone you constantly communicate with, sharing all critical information; someone you greet setbacks and roadblocks with by saying, "Let's figure out how to solve this together"; someone whose constructive comments you take graciously, offering your own in a spirit of respect, trust, and good humor. Take this exact same approach with educators: Tell Mrs. Wilson that you'll be away on business next week, in case your third-grader acts out; flag it when Susie is struggling with her Spanish homework—and ask what the best way is to support her; let the science teacher know your son loved the chemistry experiment. Teachers are professionals—

and humans. They'll notice and appreciate your collaboration, and likely respond in kind.

Remember what you're managing toward

School, with all of its deadlines, complexity, evaluations, and social pressures, can be a daunting experience, for kids and for their parents. Amid all the noise and busyness, it can be helpful to re-center by remembering the two key outcomes you—and every parent—are really shooting for: *independence* and *opportunity*. You want your son or daughter to develop into a competent, responsible adult capable of managing in a complex world. And you want them to find the maximum possible number of open doors in terms of college and, later, career. But you don't need to ensure your child has a flawless, completely bump-and-bruise-free experience at school in order to get there. It's OK—desirable, even—for your child to struggle with long division or have an argument on the playground, or for you to miss a few soccer games. These things may be upsetting in the moment, particularly to you as a high-achieving professional, but they're the experiences your child needs to become resilient, independent, and ultimately successful in their own right.

Parenting school-age children while making it happen in a full-time career can feel like an uphill marathon of a task—long, constant, and steep. But remember: School won't be the only place your child gets their education. Like all parents, you will teach your child the greatest lessons: the importance of hard work, the value of commitments to family, and the satisfaction that comes from a tough job well done.

Adapted from "How Working Parents Can Manage the Demands of School-Age Kids," on hbr.org, June 13, 2018 (product #H04DW0).

13

When Your Boss Doesn't Respect Your Family Commitments

by Rebecca Knight

Quick Takes

- Have a one-on-one conversation with your boss
- Frame your plans in terms of achieving business goals
- Communicate often—but set clear boundaries
- Find allies inside your organization
- Be ready to move on if necessary

When trying to balance your work and family commitments, it helps to have a boss who is understanding and supportive: someone who doesn't raise an eyebrow when you sign off early to attend a school event or take a personal day to accompany an aging parent to a doctor's appointment.

But what if your manager isn't sympathetic to your familial responsibilities? Or worse, your boss is outright dismissive or is even hostile toward your obligations? How should you handle a boss who refuses to acknowledge the other demands on your time? How can you find room for flexibility? What should you say about your family commitments? And who should you turn to for moral and professional support?

What the Experts Say

Too many working parents and other employees with extensive caregiving responsibilities have stories of a manager who gives them an assignment at 4 p.m. and asks for it the next morning, or a boss who makes disparaging comments about another working parent who doesn't seem loyal to the company. "There are some managers who are unsympathetic to the challenges their employees face at home and some who intentionally turn a blind eye," says Avni Patel Thompson, the founder and CEO of Modern Village, a company that provides technology solutions for parents. "Other managers may have positive intent but lack empathy or ideas on how to [support their employees]."

When you work for a manager who doesn't recognize your family obligations, your strategy must be multifaceted, says Ella F. Washington, professor at Georgetown University's McDonough School of Business and a consultant and coach at Ellavate Solutions. You need to figure out how to productively navigate the situation with your boss, while also collaborating with your colleagues and family to create a schedule and "set boundaries" that work for everyone. The goal is to "try to get your boss to meet you halfway," she says. Here are some ideas.

Know your rights

First, "know your rights" and understand what you're entitled to in terms of paid leave and care options, says Thompson. Do some research into your company's policies and whether there are alternative work arrangements on offer. An increasing number of organizations have instituted flexible work plans for employees, and many states have flex-work policies in place for their government workers. Washington recommends talking to your company's HR person, too, if you have one, to learn what options and accommodations are available to you. "Knowledge is power," she says.

Be up-front about your personal situation

Next, have a one-on-one conversation with your boss in which you are "honest and transparent about your limitations," says Thompson. Make clear your commitment to the company and your team, but also explain the additional responsibilities outside of work. After all, your manager's lack of sympathy is likely not malicious, but thoughtless. For instance, if your boss doesn't have children, they may be aware of the "superficial or obvious" tasks related to remote learning, but oblivious to the fact that parents are also serving as their kids' tech support, math tutors, writing coaches, and line cooks, says Thompson. They may not realize why a conversation with your child's teacher or guidance counselor has to take place during work hours, rather than early morning or in the evening. Explaining this to your boss may not be an easy conversation, but don't let your discomfort cause you to avoid the subject. "Silence is what makes managers nervous," warns Thompson. Remember, too, you're not throwing a woe-is-me pity party, says Washington. "This isn't about making excuses"—you're stating facts. Your tone should exude confidence and commitment.

Exhibit empathy

Summon compassion. It's not easy to be a boss. Many managers are under pressure. "They're stressed, anxious, and struggling to do more with less," says Washington. Consider the situation from their perspective.

Thompson says your empathy should be both "genuine and strategic." Ask your manager about their pain points. Find out where their worries lie. Be sincere—show you care about them as a human being—and be tactical. Ask about their "objectives and the metrics they need to hit," she says. "You'll get important information about what they're concerned about" that will help you sharpen your focus in terms of the work you prioritize.

Have a plan—or two or three

Once you "understand what's top of mind" for your manager, you can frame your plans for getting your job done in a way that helps them achieve their goals and objectives, says Thompson. Focus on results. When you're a caregiver, your schedule can often be unpredictable, so it's important to make a plan as well as several contingency ones. Address your manager's "insecurities about you not pulling your weight" by demonstrating that you're "making arrangements to get your work done." You want your manager to come away from your conversations thinking, "They've got this."

Don't be shy about reminding your manager of your track record for delivering on expectations, adds Washington. "Your past performance is the strongest indicator of your future performance," she says. Hopefully, your manager will come to see "that what's most important is not *how* the job gets done, but that it gets done."

Communicate often

Always keep your boss in the loop, says Washington. If you're not in the office, you might consider "instituting a daily check-in" or at least providing an email update every few days. "Your objective is to make your manager feel comfortable that the work is getting done," she says.

This communication doesn't require more face time though. Instead of a status update conference call, you could write an email to your team that lays out "your objectives for the week and gives visibility to what you're working on." Or in place of a team meeting on Zoom, encourage your colleagues to "collaborate on Slack," which allows you to "fire off messages even while your kids are sitting next to you."

Articulate boundaries

If your boss is a face-time tyrant, it can be tough to establish boundaries, but it's still important to do. We all need time in our day that's off-limits for work, says Washington. "If 6 p.m. is when you have dinner and put the kids down," so be it. "Have those boundaries—and let your boss know that you will be unavailable then."

But if your manager continues to be disrespectful of your family time, you need to have a conversation. Frame the discussion around you—how you prefer to structure your workday and how and when you perform best. Explain that you need your nonwork hours to regroup and take care of your family commitments. Without that time away from work, you will not be able to fully devote yourself to your job.

Broaden your network

If your direct boss continues to be difficult about your family commitments, make a concerted effort to find allies within your organization, says Thompson. These allies might include peers, colleagues in different departments, and managers outside your division. "Build relationships with people who see you for the whole life that you have," says Thompson. "That way, if down the line, things get contentious [with your boss], you've got options."

In addition to broadening your professional network, allies offer moral support, says Washington. Talk to your colleagues and find out how they're balancing their jobs with their caregiving responsibilities. "Find out how others are making this work," she says.

Take care of yourself

Working for someone who doesn't respect your life outside of work can be exhausting, so make sure you're taking time for yourself. Be purposeful about giving yourself "a forced mental break," says Thompson. Make time to read, cook, dance, run, meditate—or any other activity that you enjoy or helps you relax. "Schedule joy," she says.

And even if exercise isn't usually your thing, Thompson suggests finding time for it every day, especially during difficult periods. "Don't underestimate the power of 20–30 minutes of daily physical activity," she says. At a time when your boss is being difficult and "nothing feels in your control," getting your endorphins pumping should be a priority.

Bide your time

Even with your best efforts, the situation may not improve. In this case, Thompson's recommendation is to be the best employee you can be under the circumstances. "Make sure you deliver on expectations," she says. "Don't give your boss any ammunition" against you. Your boss might never be empathetic to your personal situation, says Washington. "If you're not getting support and the organization is not being inclusive of your needs, maybe this work environment isn't the best for your career development," she says. It may be time to move on.

Case Study #1: Know What You're Entitled to—and Be Willing to Move On

Jennifer Walden, director of operations at Wikilawn, an online company for garden professionals, says that while her current employer and manager has been flexible and accommodating regarding her family commitments, she wasn't always as fortunate.

A few years ago, when she worked in the gaming industry, her boss—we'll call him Jerry—was unsympathetic to the fact that Jennifer was a mother and that one of her children had health issues. "It was really hard," recalls Jennifer. "I remember feeling guilty because I felt I was much less productive at work when my daughter was having complications. I was constantly worried about her."

From the moment she took the job, Jennifer was open and transparent about her responsibilities at home. "I remember asking my boss early on if there were opportunities to work from home on days when my daughter's health was especially poor," she says.

Jerry said no. "He shut down any conversation having to do with remote work and flexible schedules," she says. He was overbearing and expected immediate responses to his calls and emails—even on weekends. Jennifer, meanwhile, was diligent. After a couple of months, she followed up with Jerry to plead her case. She talked about her commitment to the company and pointed to her conscientiousness and past track record of meeting her deadlines.

"I tried to alleviate his fears by being proactive in saying how I'd make up any missed work, alter my schedule, and check in regularly from home," she says.

He still didn't budge.

She began reaching out to colleagues on her team for support and encouragement. She learned that many of them had similar frustrations.

Together, they decided to talk to HR. "HR did help somewhat," she says. "I fought for the right to work from home on the days my daughter was struggling—our organization allowed this, even though my boss hadn't previously signed off."

But ultimately, the stress of working for a manager who dismissed her personal life wasn't worth it. Jennifer left the job. Her experience at Wikilawn is entirely different. "We have unlimited PTO here," she says. "My boss also frequently asks after my daughter and whether or not I need more time to get projects done when her health issues flare up."

Case Study #2: Show Your Commitment and Deliver on Expectations

Willie Greer, founder of The Product Analyst, a Memphis-based company that produces technology and product reviews, says he knows well what it feels like to have his family commitments dismissed by his boss.

A few years ago, he worked as an HR manager in the digital marketing industry. At the time, Willie had young children at home, and a spouse who also worked full-time.

When he first started at the company, he and his boss— we'll call her Sheila—had a good working relationship. Willie was a top performer, and Sheila trusted him by giving him more challenging, high-profile assignments.

But after Willie's childcare situation changed, their relationship grew tense. Willie asked if he could leave work early two days a week in order to pick up his kids from school, and Sheila turned him down. "I told her I would make up the work at night, but she said that I was needed in the office," he says.

Willie knew he needed to take action. First, he empathized with Sheila. He asked her about her priorities and concerns. She told him that she was under a lot of pressure from management and that she was particularly nervous about several looming projects.

Second, he demonstrated his commitment to the company and his job. Willie told Sheila that he would focus his attention on those projects. "I wanted her to know that the work was in safe hands," he says.

Finally, he was open and honest about his familial responsibilities. "I told her that my children were young, and that I needed a little leniency and flexibility."

Sheila wasn't enthusiastic about his request, but she agreed to a trial. Willie kept his focus on the projects and made sure that he hit every deadline. He sent Sheila regular updates and status reports to assuage her worries. And two days a week, he left work an hour early to pick up his kids.

The situation improved, but Willie still felt unhappy. "I wanted to work for a manager that values her people and who understands that there is more to life than work," he says.

He landed a new job relatively quickly, and not long after that, he founded his company. "I've created a working environment where employees can become the best versions of themselves."

Adapted from content posted on hbr.org, September 1, 2020 (product #H05UK1).

14

How to Find and Form a "Parenting Posse"

by Avni Patel Thompson

Quick Takes

- Jot down three to five areas where you need help
- Think broadly about the people who can support you
- Build new connections through virtual happy hours
- Define your support plan in practical terms
- If necessary, consider moving closer to friends and family

The beginning of 2020 was a particularly hectic one for my family. From January to March, I would fly to San Francisco every week to participate in a Y Combinator batch. It was a critical opportunity for building the digital tool Milo, but it also meant added complexity at home, with a husband building his own company and two kids in second grade and kindergarten, respectively. We had my parents as backup, but with so much going on, we knew we needed more.

I reached out to some of the parents of my daughter's friends, told them the situation, and asked if they would be able to help with some pickups or drop-offs at the school, should we need them. They readily agreed, so for two months, we had a "parenting posse" to lean on when things inevitably got sticky—a group of people that I had an explicit agreement with to serve as backup and support for a specific set of needs.

Then Covid-19 hit, and everyone's lives were turned upside down. Determined to keep some level of the posse going, I reached out to see if these same parents wanted to create a virtual pod every morning for the girls to do a math worksheet or spelling, or even just color for half an hour. Parents took turns leading, giving everyone welcome structure and community in that time.

I think often about how grateful I was to have that group—both in normal times and not. The needs were drastically different, but the intent was the same: to share the load of everyday parenting.

It's a topic that is near and dear to my heart—both in my life and also in my work. For the past five years, I've been dedicated to figuring out why the support parents have today is stuck in the last century, when the traditional definition of a family dominated, where a breadwinner brought in a "family wage," and a homemaker (typically the mother) ran everything to do with the family, from childcare to socializing. I also wanted to discover how we can build 21st-century support instead—the tools and the services that reflect the realities of today's families, whether they contain two working parents, single parents, jobs with variable work schedules, or other complex logistics. In this journey, I've thought long and hard about what it is that actually moves the needle in lightening the weight that rests on their shoulders. Turns out, it's a matter of basic physics: distribute the weight over many shoulders.

Of course, those shoulders can be hard to come by. More and more, we live in different cities than our parents and communities of our youth. And if it was difficult to find them pre-pandemic, it's nearly impossible now. We used to be worried about the regular-flavor complexity of finding the right people, fighting the feeling of imposing on them, and navigating the tricky conversations that lead to clear expectations. Now we're worried about health risks, different tolerances, and unseen burdens.

So how do you find and form a parenting posse? Whether you're navigating remote school while working from home or need a last-minute pickup from soccer practice, here are ways to create this support system.

Step 1: Identify What Help You Need Most

What are the hardest parts of your week, the proverbial straws threatening to break the camel's back? Is it needing short blocks of childcare (for key appointments, critical breaks, or important meetings), handling draining bedtimes, covering the never-ending meals (and cleanup), or dealing with feelings of isolation, lack of personal time, and little sleep? Brainstorm a list. You might discover that your list is really long, so focus on the ones that will make the biggest impact. Narrow it down to the top three to five pain points, ones that others could realistically and practically help with, without a lot of context or risk.

Step 2: Figure Out the Best People to Help You

With the most important needs in mind, make a list of all the people who could help in some way. The easiest to think of will be other parents—from your kids' school, extracurricular activities, place of worship, neighborhood, and so on. But while they certainly know the job and can help, they're also likely dealing with their own chaos. So, don't be shy about expanding beyond other parents. Are there friends or coworkers without kids, an 18-year-old neighbor attending college nearby, or a retiree with a bit of extra time on their hands?

Think expansively. When pushed, you'll be surprised at just how many people you do have in your world who are willing and able to help, especially with short, targeted requests.

Don't know a lot of people or are new to your community? Find a contact sheet from your child's school or other activities. Send out an email and suggest a virtual happy hour. It'll be a slower build, but hopefully you'll connect with a couple of people you can form a relationship with to make simple requests. Our eldest started at a new school this year, and we're taking this approach so we can meet other parents that we would otherwise be running into at pickups and drop-offs. (This approach also works if you find that you don't have time to attend in-person meet-and-greets, even when they're offered.) If you're still having trouble, choose quality over quantity, and find one family you can do the buddy system with, as outlined in the next step.

Step 3: Define Clear Systems to Get the Help You Need

With that, let's dig into what this can actually look like for your family, in practical terms. Here are four options of what your posse might look like and how it might be structured. Use them as a starting point to customize to your specific needs.

1. Kids' support and social system: Set up daily homework sessions. If the main thing you need right now is for your kids to get some social time with their friends while also doing some of their assignments (bonus: without your help), send a message to the parents of four or five kids in your child's class or grade and see if they'd be interested in doing a regular work session virtually. Find a block of 1–1.5 hours each day and send a calendar invite with a Zoom or Google Hangouts link. Have one parent supervise the group each day, leaving the other parents to serve only as backup.

2. All-purpose support: Create a buddy system. If what you need ranges from meals and socializing to breaks from the kids, then forget about the full posse and focus on just one other family to buddy up with. Decide up front what you'll help each other with—for example, shared dinners two times a week, dropping kids off at each other's house for four-hour blocks, or weekend playtime at a local park. Especially if health is a concern, look for a family that shares a similar risk tolerance as you (and you can find a safe way to get together), and the kids get along. This arrangement is far more about mutual help than it is about being best friends.

3. Parental sanity: Establish weekly calls. Don't discount the benefits of a virtual posse that helps with the mental and social-emotional side of things. Create a weekly or monthly standing session with your best friends—wherever they might live. Set up video calls or connect via WhatsApp or Marco Polo. The key is to create a space and a group that you can lean on to vent, to get reassurance, and to get ideas.

4. Community support: Create opportunities for learning and play. Find people without kids who would love to pitch in, both because they care about you, and also because they enjoy the company of kids and a broader community. It may be a coworker who has a weekly Zoom call with your kids, teaching them about a topic. It may be a college-aged neighbor who can coach your teen in tennis, or a retiree who's happy to read books to your child, virtually or in person. Likely these people will come from your already established network, but don't be afraid to see if it might be something they'd be interested in. It can't hurt to ask.

These are just a few ways you might explore finding and building your parenting posse—both in person and virtually. But if this isn't enough, go bigger.

Step 4: Explore Bigger Changes

If the pandemic has taught us anything, it's that we need to be brutally honest about our priorities. That prioritization might now include either moving to be closer to family (or bringing family to you) or relocating to a city or region where you can get more of the support you need. It's certainly not something to be done lightly and has a myriad of logistics to think through (including if your workplace is amenable to the move), but it's been a life-changing move for those who have already done it and should be an option to consider.

As I find myself saying often, There are no good choices; there is only a series of "doing our best." Finding people who help you get through the challenges of working parenthood is no different. Try one approach or try them all. See what works best for your family and the ever-changing times.

Adapted from content posted on hbr.org, October 22, 2020 (product #H05X9V).

Section 5

Home Sweet Home

Managing the House and Family

15

What's Your Family's Mission Statement?

by Priscilla Claman

Quick Takes

- Discuss the goals you want to accomplish
- Make up a phrase that reinforces your family mission
- Set achievable targets
- Revisit your goals and deadlines
- Keep the conversation going

There is no adequate word to describe the life of a working parent. Busy doesn't cut it. The stay-home-and-work-while-teaching-your-children-and-feeding-everyone-multiple-meals-a-day Tilt-A-Whirl that resulted from the Covid-19 pandemic caused many of us to stop and reassess. And, as we turn our attention to new ways of balancing our kids' school requirements and the grind of the workweek, how do we manage without getting back on the too-much-to-do treadmill?

Three common work practices can help us decide what to continue doing—and what to ditch.

Clarify Your Family Mission

I know a family who has made a tradition of goal setting. Instead of New Year's resolutions, they go around the table early in the year, and each family member mentions something they want to accomplish in the next year. It could be something momentous, like finding a new job or riding a bike without training wheels, or something simple, like knocking a few seconds off of their personal best for a 5K or setting a number of books they'd like to read in a year.

These New Year's goals are actually a part of something bigger, an overarching family mission—like the mission statement many organizations have. This family's mission is achievement: to help every member learn to achieve their own goals and to support the goals of everyone else in the family.

Your family probably has an overarching family mission, even if you haven't thought about it or spoken about it in that way. Is your family invested in addressing climate change? Your faith community? The great outdoors? Is there a phrase or family saying you use to describe yourselves to others? Those are all clues to your family's purpose.

If you don't yet have words you use regularly, make up a phrase that fits your family mission. Ask your kids what they think. Make it short so it's easy to remember and repeat. You don't need to write it down somewhere, although you could post it on your family bulletin board, if you want. Thinking about it and repeating it will help your family move in the same direction. A family mission helps you focus on what is meaningful, set priorities, and drop items that don't fit from your individual and group to-do lists.

When I was young, my family used the phrase "We never get seasick." Yes, we never actually got seasick, but what it really meant was that no matter what others were doing around you (like throwing up), you always stepped up to the challenge. You were expected to speak up and defend your position, even with your parents. That made for loud family dinners and, later, persistent adults.

My friend Christine's family mantra was "Education: It's the one thing that nobody can take away from you." Even though Christine's father died in an industrial accident when she was four, Christine's mother taught her children the family purpose, and Christine, her brothers, and sisters all graduated from high school and went on to trade school or college.

Set Short-Term SMART Goals

You probably use SMART goals at work to help create achievable targets. This is what SMART means in the working-family context:

- **S = Specific.** Instead of setting a goal with your 10-year-old to be "nicer" to your neighbor, set a goal with her to say, "Hi, Mr. Walker," when she sees him. That makes it clear to her what being nicer means to you.

- **M = Measurable.** Setting a goal with your 12-year-old to learn how to do his own laundry is easy to track and evaluate. A leaning tower of hoodies or the aroma of dirty socks shoved under his bed will indicate his progress.

- **A = Achievable.** If you set goals that feel too big or try to tackle too many goals at once, you'll grow discouraged and feel like a failure. To avoid that fate, check in with your family members before asking for their commitment: Is this something you can manage? Will you let me know if it seems like too much? How long do you think it will take you? It's an important life skill to estimate what you can do and by when. This applies to you, too. Ask yourself the same questions before you launch into a project. Speak up and offer alternatives if you aren't sure you can achieve a goal in the prescribed time.

- **R = Relevant.** Your individual goals should fit with your family's mission. I know a family whose over-arching mission is to make sure everyone learns to be independent—even their chickens are free-range. Instituting an hourly schedule with little flexibility would not fit this family's mission—or its individual goals. A homeschooling goal where family members identify topics of interest and build activities to explore further would increase the likelihood of individuals achieving their goals and serve the family mission.

- **T = Time-bound.** While family missions don't need to have an end date, SMART goals always do. Ask your 12-year-old how long it will take him to learn to do his laundry independently. If it seems reasonable to you, that's the deadline. But if his red T-shirt dyes all his other clothes pink, or if you have other reasons to think he is struggling, you might want to extend the deadline. But always have a deadline—and one he agrees to.

Revisit Your Mission If You Are Thrown Off Course

What about those well-planned goals that run into major obstacles? Although most people's first instinct is to look for a way to barrel toward their goal, it's important to stop and think things through when you encounter a setback. Ask: Do we need to recommit to our mission or purpose? Do we need to change our goals? Set new ones? When new circumstances intrude, our expectations of what we can realistically accomplish may have to change, too.

When Muriel learned she faced a yearlong treatment for breast cancer, she called a family meeting to figure out how she and her family could get through it together. Their family mission was commitment to the family— we succeed together by sticking together. By the end of the meeting, the oldest son had decided to take a year's leave from college to stay home and work nearby. The two teenaged children volunteered to cover household duties. Grandma agreed to check in with the youngest to make sure he did his homework and practiced the saxophone. Muriel's husband took on the job of personally supporting her throughout her medical treatments, arranging for Family Medical Leave with his employer for the toughest months. Their well-considered plan didn't work perfectly the whole year; it needed some rethinking and rejiggering from time to time. But the family succeeded in supporting Muriel and each other, while reinforcing their pride in working together.

Someone once told me, "You aren't really a manager until you've figured out what it is that you *don't* have to do and still be successful." These three techniques will help you redefine what life looks like as you decide what you can defer, delay, or dump. You'll still be busy. Working parents always are. But your priorities will be clear, which will reduce your stress and make you happier.

Adapted from content posted on hbr.org, August 4, 2020 (product #H05RE4).

16

Are Chore Wars at Home Holding You Back at Work?

by Rebecca Shambaugh

Quick Takes

- Let go of too-high expectations and allow imperfections
- Figure out what you want—and ask for it
- Divide the housework fairly, not evenly
- Find out what matters most to you and your partner
- Hire help if you can (and don't feel bad about it)

J ane is a marketing director at a technology firm, where she manages a small team, works late, and travels once per quarter. Her husband, Paul, runs his own landscaping business, which often requires working long hours six days a week. (I've changed their names and some details.) At the start of their marriage, four years ago, the couple agreed that because they had equally demanding jobs, they each would be responsible for certain chores around the house.

But as time went on, Jane found herself doing all of the housework except for mowing the lawn. On Paul's days off from work, Jane noticed with exasperation that he would just lie on the couch. Trying to keep up with the cleaning, cooking, and laundry each week left her with practically no free time to devote to herself, either personally or professionally. "I would feel like I was being selfish by spending that time on my career—for example, by staying late at the office to finish an important project—rather than doing something I knew needed to be done around the house," she told me.

Jane isn't alone—far from it. As a leadership coach, I work with many female leaders and managers on improving their time management skills and work-life balance.

Why split hairs over something as seemingly trivial as housework? Because once you home in on exactly how many hours you're devoting to it, you might be surprised just how much time you're losing. By taking on too many household responsibilities while men use their free time to recharge and advance their careers, women can lose sight of their priorities and fail to move ahead in areas that are most important to them.

Although American men today do more housework than past generations, they still aren't doing as much as their wives. This translates directly into men having more leisure time and more time at the office, while their wives have less.[1] Even being a breadwinner doesn't exempt women from household chores. A study from McKinsey and LeanIn.org found that "women in senior management are seven times more likely than men at the same level to say they do more than half of the housework."[2] Women who outearn their husbands actually end up doing more housework than their spouses.[3] (Note: Some studies suggest that the chore wars are an American phenomenon. Couples in other countries are sometimes more egalitarian—in France, men do more housework than women.[4])

Housework: Another "Sticky Floor"?

Both genders play a role in creating this predicament. It isn't just that men are failing to step up and lighten women's loads; a study from the University of Michigan shows that in heterosexual married couples, husbands are actually *adding* seven weekly hours of housework to their wives' plates.[5] Women, on the other hand, were shown to save their husbands from an hour of household chores every week. But women's failure to recognize their own limits in the work-life juggle is one of several, what I have coined, "sticky floors"—self-limiting beliefs and behaviors that can hold women back from achieving their professional goals that I identify in my book *It's Not a Glass Ceiling, It's a Sticky Floor.* This is because the root cause of chronic work-life imbalance can be linked to overly high standards, a reluctance to delegate, a skewed sense of loyalty, a refusal to set reasonable boundaries, or some combination of these factors:

- **Overly high standards.** Those who demand perfection from themselves at work may place similar pressures on their jobs around the house. By insisting on having housework done "just right," they may inadvertently stick themselves with the task since no one else can measure up to their level of cleanliness and detail. Again, this may be an American thing—American women report spending much more time on household tasks than women in Australia, Japan, Brazil, Spain, and France, for example.[6]

- **Skewed sense of loyalty.** Some women hold themselves to high standards not out of a sense of perfectionism but because they feel that they aren't good enough, in their roles at work or at home, and overcompensate to try to make up for their perceived shortcomings. I've coached many talented executive women who turn introspection and self-examination into a continuous mental loop of self-criticism. As a result, they might find themselves taking on more than their fair share of duties around the house (and lower-level tasks in the office), trying to prove that they're a devoted wife, or mother, or worker, rather than asking for what they need to accomplish their larger goals.

- **Reluctance to delegate.** We all know people who struggle to delegate, but we rarely find it easy to recognize this trait in ourselves. You may think that you can "do it all," but research shows that your effectiveness declines when you over-task.[7] Women need to be particularly cognizant of this fact since they multitask more frequently than men.[8]

- **Lack of reasonable boundaries.** Sometimes the wife ends up doing the majority of the housework not because she's a perfectionist or a martyr but simply because someone has to do it, and it's easier to just do something than to nag someone else. And many women are proud to be hardworking employees, spouses, and parents. But trying to do everything for everyone leaves little time for themselves and their own careers. Like Jane in the example earlier, women can end up feeling resentful toward those who help perpetuate this pattern. "It's gotten to the point that I sometimes outright resent my husband for being able to rest all day on the days he has off, whereas if I'm home and not doing something around the house, I somehow feel less," explains Jane.

Banishing the "Angel in the House"

What I've come to realize through coaching clients like Jane is that for many executive women, the key to cracking the time management code at work starts at home, with something as basic as division of labor around household chores.

As a woman and working mom, you must focus on your priorities and give yourself permission to let a few balls drop. It's OK to get the resources you need, whether from family members or outsourcing, to spend more time on the things that really matter to you. While there are no easy answers, successful resolution to the chore wars depends on effective negotiation, couple by couple; what works for one pair may leave others dissatisfied. Here are some strategies to try out with your partner:

- **Give yourself permission to do what *you* need.** When women try to be all things to all people and put themselves last, no one wins. If you're in this situation, figure out what you want the most—a more helpful partner, a hired hand, or simply a break from the grind—and begin by asking for it without feeling guilty. You may not get what you want right away, but if you're not even asking, you'll never receive it. (And for any men reading, step up. Many women are used to bending to their partner's preferences, but if men can do the same, it can save their marriages.[9])

- **Negotiate for *fair*, not *even*.** While your sense of justice may push for a perfect divide between household tasks so that each spouse takes on exactly half of the burden, a study conducted by Norwegian researchers showed that couples who split housework 50/50 were more likely to divorce.[10] The lesson is that your partner might interpret insisting on a perfect division of labor as "keeping score." As an alternative, seek fair—but not necessarily even—task distribution so that you both feel that you are putting equal effort into the home.

- **Figure out your own form of "marriage insurance."**
  Tell your partner what specific actions would make
  the biggest difference to you—steps that would be
  real game changers if your spouse were to start
  doing these things regularly. Commit to your own
  form of marriage insurance by finding out what
  matters most to both of you, and see if you can find
  common ground to get these needs met.

- **Don't feel guilty if you decide to hire help.** To
  break the stalemate, some couples may opt to hire
  help, but be aware that this isn't always a stress-free
  solution. There can still be tension about whose
  chores are being outsourced or how to pay for it.
  You may need to negotiate to find the right balance, but the bottom line is, if the stakes are too
  high and emotionally charged to get the work done
  for free—and if it's affordable for your family to
  hire help to stop the chore wars—it will be worth
  every penny.

Relief from the chore wars can allow women to become more resilient, focused, and intentional about their
most important goals—both at home and at work.

Adapted from content posted on hbr.org, January 19, 2017 (product #H03ET8).

17

Finding Balance as a Dual-Career Couple

by Amy Jen Su

Quick Takes

- Think of your family as a team—and give it a name
- Say no to activities that don't add value
- Divvy up tasks according to strengths and interests
- Schedule regular "look-ahead" meetings
- Create boundaries for discussing and doing work at home

According to research from the Bureau of Labor Statistics, nearly half of marriages in the United States are composed of dual-career couples.[1] That number rises to 63% in married couples with children. Kids or no kids, the advantages of a dual-career household—including greater financial stability and a chance for both partners to pursue career fulfillment—are significant.

Yet dual-career couples face a unique set of challenges and trade-offs. In my role as an executive coach, it's becoming increasingly common for these clients to seek advice concerning not just the workplace but the home as well. When both you and your partner have busy, demanding careers, how can you reap the benefits of being a dual-career couple and show up as your best self, at work and at home?

Negotiating whose career takes prominence at any given time, juggling two work schedules and household and family duties, and maintaining healthy boundaries between home life and work life are often the most difficult areas to navigate. While each household is different, the couples I've seen overcome these challenges have developed systems that optimize their time and energy—as a unit. Below are some of the most successful practices my clients have put into action.

Think of Your Family as a Team

When you have a demanding career, it can be easy to become so wrapped up in your work that your time at home gets shuffled down the priority list. To overcome this, you need to give your family or partner the same level of dedication that you give to your team at work.

Coming up with a name for your home team—or your family—is a fun way to shift your mindset. Doing so can help remind you and your partner that it should never be "my career versus your career." Rather, you should view yourselves as allies. One leader I worked with and his wife—who also had a successful career—chose the name "Team Quinn" after their family surname. Another couple picked the acronym GBG, which stood for "Go Bernsteins Go."

These names helped them see each other more fully as partners navigating day-to-day challenges, just as they do with their colleagues at work. Team Quinn began planning a home schedule as a unit—accounting for career demands, the kids' activities, and fun family outings. In doing so, they were able to reduce the resentments that often arise when dual-career couples fail to work together.

Get Comfortable Saying No

As your and your partner's careers advance, you may gain more influence and receive an increasing number of requests beyond your day-to-day work responsibilities. You may be invited to attend client dinners, join boards, speak at events, or even become mentors. These activities are often rewarding, but they require time and energy. To maintain a healthy work-life equation, you'll need to get comfortable saying no. But knowing when to turn down a request isn't always easy.

One professional I worked with offers an example. She felt an obligation to join her son's school board because she wanted to be involved in supporting his education, and many of her colleagues had done the same for their children. But the more we explored the issue, the more it became clear that taking on this role was more of a "should" than a "want to." Ultimately, it would tip the scales of what was already a tight situation at home.

My client considered the value-add of her options. She could spend her time outside of work with the parents and teachers on the board, or she could use it for quality time with her son. She and her spouse chose the latter. By having an honest conversation about what was important to them, they were able to work around their schedules and show up for their son in a way that worked best for the entire family.

To find the work-life equation that supports your best self, you'll need to do the same. Carefully consider the value-add of each request you receive by asking yourself the following questions:

- Is it something for which you can uniquely add value?

- Will you derive value by attending or joining?

- What would be the impact on your spouse and home team?

The reality is, you can't do it all—and neither can your partner. That's why every request you accept should have a significant value-add.

Play to Each Other's Strengths and Interests

With both partners working, staying on top of household and family responsibilities is a continuous struggle. More often than not, you have to be strategic and disciplined about who does what, especially as your work and family roles grow.

Divvying up responsibilities according to each other's strengths and interests can be a lifesaver. One couple I consulted was in constant conflict due to the stresses of juggling household duties. To ease the tension, I had them list their responsibilities—everything from unloading the dishwasher to managing bills to getting their kids to and from extracurriculars. Next, I asked them to categorize each item on the list as "loathe," "don't mind," or "enjoy." The couple was then able to reassign items based on each person's strengths and interest levels, dramatically decreasing tension and maximizing their capacity to be effective and present. If you find that a few items on your own list are important but loathsome to both you and your partner, outsourcing can be a tremendously helpful option.

Schedule Regular "Look-Ahead" Meetings

There will inevitably be times when you and your partner have to negotiate expectations and make decisions about whose career takes the front seat. To do this, dual-career couples need to be in constant communication. A simple solution is to schedule regular look-ahead meetings to plan and set expectations. These meetings are times for open, honest communication, which will help you both stay actively involved in big decisions about career changes, projects, or goals.

The following items are a few time frames to follow. Use the ones that work best for you and your partner:

- **Annually:** Once a year, look ahead and block off vacations, school performances, conferences, and other important events you know are coming up.

- **Quarterly/monthly:** Once a month, plan for upcoming travel, deadlines, or busy work periods.

- **Weekly:** Once a week, discuss your plan for the days ahead to minimize surprises and frustrations.

In addition to keeping you and your partner on the same page, look-ahead meetings are great times to ask each other for support. If you have a critical presentation and need more time to prepare, or if your partner is anticipating an especially busy week, a look-ahead allows you both to plan and prepare. When the unexpected arises, as it inevitably will, you'll already know what's on tap for each other. As a result, you'll be able to more easily pivot and support the spouse who's in crunch time.

Create "Time Zones" and "Home Zones"

Maintaining clear boundaries between work and home can be especially challenging for dual-career couples. Many of my clients experience guilt about what's going on at home while they're at work, and fight the urge to pick up their laptops and complete a work task while they're at home. One way to break this cycle is to create "time zones" and "home zones."

Time zones are blocks of productive work time. They can also be used to denote when you and your partner will discuss work, rather than letting it leak into every conversation. For example, one professional I coached added the following time zones to her and her spouse's Saturday schedule:

- 9 a.m. to 10 a.m.: Have breakfast together, be fully present.

- 10 a.m. to noon: One partner catches up on work (Time zone #1).

- 1 p.m. to 3 p.m.: The other partner catches up on work (Time zone #2).

- 3 p.m.: Have fun with friends or family for the rest of the day.

Home zones, on the other hand, are the physical spaces in your house—such as an office or a den—used to get a little extra work done or crank through those emails. Designating certain spaces for work serves as a powerful boundary between work life and home life, and helps reinforce expectations: When a partner is in the home zone, their time and availability are protected, and vice versa.

It's worth remembering that work and home aren't in opposition—they're different aspects of life that constantly inform and influence each other. Succeeding as a dual-career couple in a way that enables both partners to be their best selves requires regularly examining your operating system. By keeping it intentional and updated, you will increase the probability of reaping the many opportunities your situation can bring.

Adapted from content posted on hbr.org, July 29, 2019 (product #H052KL).

18

How Working Parents Feed Their Families

Contributed by 19 HBR readers

Quick Takes

- Plan, plan, and plan ahead
- Create solid routines
- Let your children be the chefs
- Limit your options to make decision making easier
- Treat yourself to an occasional meal club or takeout
- Rethink what makes a meal

Editor's Note: You know how difficult it is to get food on the table for your family. One child will only eat peanut butter, one refuses to eat anything green, and another just announced they're going vegan. And while the biggest stressors used to be packing lunches before school and squeezing in dinner between extracurriculars and bedtime, the recent pandemic has now put food prep and cleanup top of mind 24/7. Breakfast, lunch, dinner, snacks—what can you do to make sure everyone is fed and happy?

To help you, we reached out to our LinkedIn community to find out what tips and tricks they use to get food on the table, despite their busy schedules. Here is a selection of their responses to spark new ideas for you and to offer you some creative ways to feed your family—without the headaches.

Plan ahead—most of the time

My wife and I try our best to do as much prep as possible the night before. You generally know what to expect tomorrow regarding activities and schedules—minus unexpected emergencies—so you can be adequately prepared 80% of the time. That last 20% you can address with healthy takeout options, previously prepared and frozen food, or on-the-go prepackaged snacks.

—**HASSAN A.**, father of three, USA

Have an established menu

After they're showered and dressed, the guys come down for either a hot or cold breakfast. We have cereal and toast daily, but a few times a week we do eggs. We make sandwiches for lunch, and the boys add in the sides. We always have fruit and veggies as well as yogurt and other snacks. The key to it all is *routine*; this makes each day easy, and no one asks what is for breakfast or lunch.

—**MARIA H.**, mother of three, USA

Set expectations

We do a weekly menu plan and include our little one in the process. This ensures that she knows what's coming and that her favorites are included. We also try to include her in meal prep (usually dinner or weekend breakfast), so that she is involved in the process of creating her meal. Because of this, her tastes have gotten more adventurous. The menu plan also means that we shop once a week, and we're not struggling day-to-day to figure out what to cook or what she is open to eating.

—**AMNAH M.**, mother of one, England

Prepare staples in batches

Make extra of anything and repurpose it for future meals. For hot, homemade breakfasts, make pancakes and waffles in extra-large batches. You can easily double or triple the recipe listed on the box and then store them in the freezer. Kids can reheat them in the microwave, toaster, or toaster oven before school.

For other staples, I make an extra-large batch of pasta to use as side dishes. Add butter and garlic one night, pasta sauce another, Alfredo another night, and so on. Do the same with rice. A super-large batch is enough for three meals to use as a side dish with simple butter and salt, teriyaki sauce, soy sauce, lemon garlic sauce, and so on.

—**TRISHA S.**, mother of one, USA

Have "forgot to shop" meals

We regularly have cheese and bread or chips handy to create the "last-minute forgot to shop" meals for lunch or dinner. For example: grilled cheese sandwiches, loaded nachos (canned black beans with salsa, too), open-faced avocado toast when in season, and cheese melted on potatoes, broccoli, and other frozen vegetables, with chips and salsa on the side when available.

—**RAY C.**, father of three, USA

Share responsibility

Plan a menu in advance, shop online, and involve the kids. Everyone has access to our online shopping app so if something runs out, it can be added to the shopping list right away. We're each responsible for our own breakfast, and lunch can be chosen from healthy fresh options in the fridge. The kids have an assigned night to make dinner, too, so they choose a recipe in advance and, with parent supervision, are learning to cook. Getting food on the table doesn't have to be onerous. We have found a way to make it fun!

—**NICKI B.**, mother of two, Canada

For younger kids, make cooking a spectator sport

I have a 2-year-old and a 5-year-old, a full-time job, and a restaurateur for a husband, so most childcare falls on me outside of crèche. Dinnertime is our time, so I'll often have one kid on the stepladder and one on the counter where I'm making the food, and I let them help and taste where they can, as I talk them through what I'm doing. Those are the meals that they wolf down!

—**JESSICA N.**, mother of two, South Africa

Let diners customize their meals

I live with my extended family part-time and regularly cook meals for seven, including my two nieces, ages 5 and 7. Here is what helps: Make it customizable. Make things like taco bowls where everyone can add their own meat or vegetables. It is so helpful!

—**MEGAN S.**, aunt of two, USA

Make it a competition

One of my favorite emerging traditions in our household is the Friday Leftover Lunch Challenge. Everyone gets one star for each leftover consumed during lunch break. It's a fun bit of silly competition and cleans out all of the odds and ends from our fridge before the weekend.

—**KELLY H.P.**, mother of three, USA

Streamline your decision making

I was a single father of five way back when. After working a very full day, my biggest challenge was dinner. I had no issue with cooking, but I found I would get stuck making the decision about what to make. So I created index cards with all of the meals we would typically eat—probably 25 or so. When dinner time came, I would just grab the top one off the pile and off we went to make dinner. It was a game changer for me, and it made sure we ate (mostly) healthy food and maintained some variety.

—**GABRIEL C.**, father of five, USA

Join a meal club

We struggled to get our kids to contribute to the cooking and appreciate dinner on the table until we joined a meal club. We have meals sent two times per week that include a recipe and the ingredients. The kids are responsible for these meals. It has been a great way to give them responsibility, and it has taught them how to cook a lot of different things. It has been a game changer!

—**ALLYSON K.**, mother of two, USA

Change your cooking schedule

I work from home, so I cook dinner at 2:30—when my kids get home from school, they interrupt my day anyway. Then when they shuffle back out for sports, I work again. When they get home starving, dinner is ready!

—**WENDY W.**, mother of two, USA

Give your pantry a makeover

While we do well with dinner when we finish work, lunch is do-it-yourself since we all eat at different times. We found the kids were happy to learn how to make sandwiches and macaroni and cheese, only for us to realize (to our horror) that, left to their own devices, kids will have multiple meals of macaroni and cheese a day—and even every day.

That led us to clean up the pantry, removing the easy-to-make stuff, and actually teaching our kids to cook basics such as rice, eggs, hot sandwiches, and even salads. It has also helped them gauge how hungry they are. Kids tend to do quick and easy foods when they're bored and cook more wholesome meals when they're actually hungry.

—**MIGUEL C.**, father of two, USA

Create one-on-one experiences

I've taken to cooking with each of my kids, one night a week. This gives us some one-on-one time, where I get to really hear about how they're doing. We make it fun. They get to choose the music, and we choose the recipes together. This hour of downtime with each of my kids is something we look forward to. We've given up on any regular breakfast or lunch (we just snack all day), but dinner is when we come together.

—**VIDYA D.**, mother of three, USA

Outsource meals where you can

We decided to send our child to a school serving breakfast and lunch that offered a variety of healthy, nutritious food the whole week. For dinner, we have homecooked food—mostly vegetarian—and once a week, lunch at a restaurant.

—**UMA N.**, mother of one, India

Make "dinnertime" snack time

No one in my family follows the same diet. I try to find neat snacks and create opportunities for diversity with our nightly "Quarantine Snack," which is the final meal of the night. Everyone gets something a little different, but there are always nuts and fruit, veggies, Jell-O, sometimes baked goods, and other times chips. Turkey pepperoni and cheese cubes also make the feature list often. I don't remember the last time we sat at the table either. We've conformed to a new way of thinking: Our connection doesn't always come around the table; it comes in other new ways.

—**KAIT D.**, mother of one, Canada

Separate cooking and cleaning

Whoever cooks dinner does not clean; if you don't cook, you're on cleaning duty. You also need to establish clarity around what it means to "clean" the kitchen. My husband and son had different definitions, until they listed out all the tasks together and agreed on who does what on the nights they clean.

—**MEREDITH S.**, mother two, USA

Let go (and order out)

I made food a priority but was willing to abandon plans in lieu of takeout, so we could be sure to spend time together.

—**ANNA T.**, mother of two, USA

Epilogue

Nobody's
Perfect

19

Lessons from a Working Mom on "Doing It All"

by Francesca Gino

Quick Takes

- Be happy, not perfect
- Find the upside in mistakes
- Focus on what makes sense for *you*
- Laugh more often

"I don't know how you do it." Whether it comes at the start of a videoconference or a call, this is one of the most frequent comments I hear from clients, colleagues, and even friends these days as we're doing our usual premeeting check-ins.

The statement always surprises me. I'm a professor who teaches and a consultant who advises various organizations, in person and virtually. I am a researcher, engaged with colleagues on several projects. I am a partner, married to a committed working spouse, and I am the mom of four children: the oldest is seven; the youngest is just over six months old. When I hear "I don't know how you do it," my answer is "I don't!"—at least not perfectly and sometimes not even well.

Like me, many working adults across the globe have been juggling a lot, especially since the Covid-19 crisis started. I've heard many people complain about their difficult realities and bad experiences, and certainly many are facing extreme challenges. But, for those of us managing more minor struggles, I've come to believe that the difference between going to bed feeling content or disappointed at the end of the day has a lot to do with the expectations we set for ourselves. Let's lower our standards. Better yet: Let's use this moment to shift them to something more reasonable.

Here is how I've done it, by focusing on four simple principles.

Go for Happy, Not Perfect

A lot of us can identify with—and have benefited from—the desire to be perfect. But we often take it too far. Even before the pandemic, research by personality psychologists Thomas Curran and Andrew Hill found that growing numbers of people were struggling to match unreachable ideals. The two psychologists studied more than 40,0000 American, British, and Canadian college students between 1989 and 2016 and found that perfectionism has increased dramatically over the last few decades—33% since 1989.[1] We seem to be internalizing a contemporary myth that life should be perfect, when, in fact, that is an impossible outcome and can contribute to serious anxiety and depression. Those who become preoccupied with perfection set themselves up for failure and psychological turmoil.

Instead of aiming for perfection, we need to aim for happiness. I remind myself that this is the goal every single day. I'm patient if it takes me longer than expected to get work done. And, at the dinner table every evening, I ask my little ones to talk about what made them happy and what they feel grateful for that day.

Accept Mistakes with Curiosity

In the middle of a busy night at the celebrated restaurant Osteria Francescana in Modena, Italy, one of the sous chefs, Taka, jumped in to make desserts after the pastry chef's abrupt departure. As he assembled some lemon tarts, one accidentally fell to the ground. Taka froze as the restaurant's chef and owner, Massimo Bottura, saw the mess. But instead of getting upset, Bottura was inspired. Today, one of the most popular desserts on the restaurant's menu is called "Oops! I dropped the lemon tart." It is carefully constructed to look like a mess: A light and foamy zabaglione is splashed over lemon cubes, bergamot jelly, spiced apple, a few drops of chili and lemon oil, and honeyed capers from an island off the coast of Sicily, and it's topped by a lemongrass sorbet and a broken biscuit.

These days, I take solace in this story. Rarely do my days go as planned. One of my four children may unexpectedly interrupt a work Zoom call, or some emergency requires me to drop a paper in the middle of a sentence—even when it turns out the yelling across the room was simply prompted by me preparing a different lunch than I had promised. I am striving to be more like Bottura, looking at mistakes and accidents with a curious mind.

Focus on What Makes Sense for *You*

While working on my book *Rebel Talent*, I met Captain Chesley "Sully" Sullenberger, the pilot who managed to land a commercial aircraft safely in the Hudson River on a cold January day in 2009 when both engines failed. Sully looked beyond the most obvious option (landing at the nearest airport) to come up with a more creative and promising solution.

Especially when we're under pressure, we narrow in on what immediately seems like the best course of action. But a better approach is to contemplate a wide range of options and perspectives. Take all the advice we hear about the importance of getting a good night's sleep to our health and well-being. Well, I can't remember the last time I slept for more than a few uninterrupted hours or beyond 6 a.m., due to nightmares, trips to the bathroom with one of my oldest three, or my 4-year-old strangely announcing she can't find her bed at 3 a.m. And that's OK: I now laugh at the recommendations on sleep, since they clearly don't apply to me right now. I have colleagues who have told me that they have never been more productive than when the pandemic started, and friends who have never been in better shape or better rested. That's not what I've experienced, and that's OK. I smile at their accomplishments and laugh at the fact that exercise, these days, is often running around the house after my kids. That brings me to my last principle.

Find Time for Laughter

Everyone enjoys a good laugh, but who actually makes time for it? We all may agree that listening to a funny joke, talking to people with a good sense of humor, and watching comedies are all pleasant activities, but do we block out space in our calendar for them? Especially during crises, we should do just that because amusement has lots of benefits. According to a 2015 study, the act of laughing makes us more open to new people and helps us build relationships.[2] It can also help us regulate our emotions in the face of challenge, according to a study led by Yale psychologist Erica J. Boothby.[3] Laughter can improve our health and make us better learners. And what's more: Laughter is contagious.[4]

Despite all the negativity in the today's news, it shouldn't take much to find something to laugh at. This morning, when I repeatedly asked my 3-year-old to please put her underwear on before going outside and then found my 4-year-old painting herself instead of a canvas, I let myself laugh rather than getting upset.

After a couple of weeks in lockdown, my husband and I noticed that we would sometimes find ourselves on a short fuse, snapping with criticism that didn't really need to be aired. Our solution? We decided that if one of us wanted to criticize the other (for example, "You could have put the dishes in the dishwasher rather than leaving them in the sink"), we would do so while dancing in a goofy manner, turning a stressful moment into a light-hearted one.

So many situations are out of our control. But we do have choices about how we approach each day and the expectations we set for ourselves. Now is the time to follow these principles and find a little more peace.

Adapted from content posted on hbr.org, June 25, 2020 (product #H05P80).

NOTES

Chapter 1

1. "Raising Kids and Running a Household: How Working Parents Share the Load," Pew Research Center, November 4, 2015, https://www.pewsocialtrends.org/2015/11/04/raising-kids-and-running-a-household-how-working-parents-share-the-load/.

Chapter 2

1. M. Hoghughi and A. N. P. Speight, "Good Enough Parent for All Children—A Strategy for a Healthier Society," *Archives of Disease in Childhood* 78, no. 4 (1998): 293–296.

Chapter 3

1. Loes Meeussen and Colette Van Laar, "Feeling Pressure to Be a Perfect Mother Relates to Parental Burnout and Career Ambitions," *Frontiers in Psychology* 9, no. 2113 (2013).

2. Catherine Caruso, "Pregnancy Causes Lasting Changes in a Woman's Brain," *Scientific American*, December 19, 2016, https://www.scientificamerican.com/article/pregnancy-causes-lasting-changes-in-a-womans-brain/.

Chapter 4

1. "When Everyone Can Work from Home, What's the Office For?," PWC Remote Work Survey, June 25, 2020, https://www.pwc.com/us/en/library/covid-19/assets/pwc-return-to-work-survey.pdf.

Chapter 6

1. Adam Grant and Sheryl Sandberg, "Madam C.E.O., Get Me a Coffee," *New York Times*, February 6, 2015, https://www.nytimes

.com/2015/02/08/opinion/sunday/sheryl-sandberg-and-adam
-grant-on-women-doing-office-housework.html.

Chapter 9

1. H. R. 5065, Bottles and Breastfeeding Equipment Screening
Act, 114th Congress, December 16, 2016, https://www.congress
.gov/bill/114th-congress/house-bill/5065/text.

Chapter 16

1. Amanda Marcotte, "Even When They Don't Have Jobs, Men
Do Less Housework Than Women," Slate, January 6, 2015, https://
slate.com/human-interest/2015/01/gender-and-housework-even
-men-who-don-t-work-do-less-than-women.html; "85 Percent of
Women, 67 Percent of Men, Spent Time Doing Household Activities on Average Day in 2015," U.S. Bureau of Labor Statistics,
June 30, 2016, https://www.bls.gov/opub/ted/2016/85-percent
-of-women-67-percent-of-men-spent-time-doing-household
-activities-on-average-day-in-2015.htm.

2. "Women in the Workplace 2016," McKinsey & Company and
Lean In (2016), https://wiw-report.s3.amazonaws.com/Women_in
_the_Workplace_2016.pdf.

3. Olga Khazan, "Emasculated Men Refuse to Do Chores—Except
Cooking," *Atlantic*, October 24, 2016, https://www.theatlantic
.com/health/archive/2016/10/the-only-chore-men-will-do-is-cook/
505067/.

4. Yasemin Besen-Cassino and Dan Cassino, "Division of House
Chores and the Curious Case of Cooking," *About Gender* 3, no. 6
(2014).

5. "Husbands Create 7 Hours of Extra Housework for Their
Wives," *Huffpost*, February 19, 2016, https://www.huffpost.com/
entry/husbands-create-7-hours-of-extra-housework-for-their
-wives_n_56c72146e4b0ec6725e23e2c?guccounter=2.

6. Besen-Cassino and Cassino, "Division of House Chores."

7. Beth Cabrera, "Women Need Mindfulness Even More Than Men Do," *Harvard Business Review*, June 21, 2016, https://hbr.org/2016/06/women-need-mindfulness-even-more-than-men-do.

8. Shira Offer and Barbara Schneider, "Revisiting the Gender Gap in Time-Use Patterns," *American Sociological Review* 76, no. 6 (2011): 809-833.

9. Zach Brittle, "Manage Conflict: Accepting Influence," Gottman Institute, April 29, 2015, https://www.gottman.com/blog/manage-conflict-accepting-influence/.

10. Jenna Goudreau, "Could Sharing Housework Equally Send You to Divorce Court?," *Forbes*, October 2012, https://www.forbes.com/sites/jennagoudreau/2012/10/05/could-sharing-housework-equally-send-you-to-divorce-court/?sh=647bdf867472.

Chapter 17

1. Bureau of Labor Statistics, "Employment Characteristics of Families—2019", press release, April 21, 2020, https://www.bls.gov/news.release/pdf/famee.pdf.

Chapter 19

1. Thomas Curran and Andrew P. Hill, "Perfectionism Is Increasing Over Time," *Psychological Bulletin*, 145, no. 4 (2019): 4019–429.

2. Alan W. Gray, Brian Parkinson, and Robin I. Dunbar, "Laughter's Influence on the Intimacy of Self-Disclosure," *Human Nature* 26 (2015): 28–43.

3. Erica J. Boothby, Margaret S. Clark, and John A. Bargh, "Shared Experiences Are Amplified," *Psychological Science* 25, no. 12 (2014).

4. Jane E. Warren et al., "Positive Emotions Preferentially Engage an Auditory-Motor 'Mirror' System," *Journal of Neuroscience* 26, no. 50 (2006).

ABOUT THE CONTRIBUTORS

DAISY DOWLING, SERIES EDITOR, is the founder and CEO of Workparent, the executive coaching and training firm, and the author of *Workparent: The Complete Guide to Succeeding on the Job, Staying True to Yourself, and Raising Happy Kids* (Harvard Business Review Press, 2021). She is a full-time working parent to two young children. She can be reached at www.workparent.com.

JULIA BECK is the founder of the It's Working Project and Forty Weeks. A passionate strategist, storyteller, and connector, she is based in Washington, D.C., where she is the matriarch of a blended family that includes a loving husband, a loyal golden retriever, and four children—all of whom are her favorite. Find her @TheJuliaBeck.

SUZANNE BROWN is a work-life balance speaker, consultant, and author of the award-winning books *Mompowerment* and *The Mompowerment Guide to Work-Life Balance*. She helps companies become more balance-friendly and working moms create greater work-life balance. Find more practical tips to shift your mindset about balance and take action on www.mompowerment.

com. In her downtime, you can find her on a nearby hiking trail or far-off adventure with her husband and their two young boys.

PRISCILLA CLAMAN is a retired human resources executive and consultant. She is a contributor to the *HBR Guide to Getting the Right Job.* In addition to coaching many people through periods of corporate craziness, she survived a week with three children under 2 and a broken washing machine. Besides her three children, she has 9 grandchildren and is a supplemental parent to 4 dogs, 2 cats, a rabbit, a retired horse, and 11 chickens.

AMY GALLO is a contributing editor at *Harvard Business Review* and the author of the *HBR Guide to Dealing with Conflict* (Harvard Business Review Press, 2017). She writes and speaks about workplace dynamics. As the parent of a teenager, she spends a lot of time trying to figure out how to apply her own advice to difficult conversations at home. Follow her on Twitter @amyegallo.

FRANCESCA GINO is a behavioral scientist and the Tandon Family Professor of Business Administration at Harvard Business School. She is the author of the books *Rebel Talent* and *Sidetracked: Why Our Decisions Get Derailed, and How We Can Stick to the Plan.* Follow her on Twitter @francescagino.

REBECCA KNIGHT is a freelance journalist in Boston whose work has been published in the *New York Times*, *USA Today*, and the *Financial Times*. She is the mom of two tweenage daughters.

DEBORAH M. KOLB is the Deloitte Ellen Gabriel Professor for Women in Leadership (Emerita) and a cofounder of the Center for Gender in Organizations at Simmons College School of Management. An expert on negotiation and leadership, she is codirector of The Negotiations in the Workplace Project at the Program on Negotiation at Harvard Law School. She and Jessica L. Porter are coauthors of *Negotiating at Work: Turn Small Wins into Big Gains*.

JANNA KORETZ, PSY.D, is a psychologist and the founder of Azimuth, which provides therapy focused on the unique mental health challenges of individuals in high-pressure careers. As the mother of a 1-year-old, Janna spends a lot of time each day getting her webcam angle just right so that the growing mess behind her cannot be seen by her colleagues.

MARINA MULTHAUP is a student at Harvard Law School and former research and policy fellow for the Center for WorkLife Law at the University of California, Hastings College of the Law.

PALENA NEALE is the founder of unabridged, a leadership coaching, mentoring, and consulting practice focused on helping women use their power and potential for greater personal and social impact. She researches and teaches on the topics of women's leadership, and in her nonwork time spends time with family spread across three continents. Follow her on Twitter @PalenaNeale.

JESSICA L. PORTER is the coauthor (with Deborah M. Kolb) of the book *Negotiating at Work: Turn Small Wins into Big Gains* and was the lead researcher of *Sleeping with Your Smartphone: How to Break the 24/7 Habit and Change the Way You Work,* by Leslie A. Perlow. In addition to her research and writing, she consults to create change around issues of leadership development, team communication and learning, and organization development. She works with corporations and organizations to develop customized programs and strategies to help ensure the advancement of talented women.

REBECCA SHAMBAUGH is an internationally recognized leadership expert, author, and keynote speaker. She's president of SHAMBAUGH, a global leadership development organization whose mission is to create inclusive work cultures that drive greater talent utilization, innovation, and gender balance. Rebecca is founder of

Women in Leadership and Learning (WILL), one of the first executive leadership development programs in the country dedicated to the research, advancement, and retention of women leaders and executives.

AMY JEN SU is a cofounder and managing partner of Paravis Partners, a premier executive coaching and leadership development firm. For the past two decades, she has coached CEOs, executives, and rising stars in organizations. She is the author of the Harvard Business Review Press book *The Leader You Want to Be* and coauthor of *Own the Room* with Muriel Maignan Wilkins. Amy is also a full-time working parent with a teenage son who is currently in high school.

AVNI PATEL THOMPSON is the founder and CEO of Modern Village. She is a third-time founder building technology solutions for today's parents. Her previous company, Poppy (YC W16), helped connect parents to vetted caregivers when they had gaps in childcare. Before taking the entrepreneurial plunge, she spent over a decade building big consumer businesses at P&G, adidas, and Starbucks. She has an MBA from Harvard Business School and a BSc in Chemistry from the University of British Columbia. She lives in Vancouver, Canada, with her husband and two little girls.

JOAN C. WILLIAMS is a professor and the founding director of the Center for WorkLife Law at the University of California's Hastings College of the Law. Her newest book is *White Working Class: Overcoming Class Cluelessness in America* (Harvard Business Review Press, 2017).

SHERYL G. ZIEGLER, PSY.D, is the author of *Mommy Burnout: How to Reclaim Your Life and Raise Healthier Children in the Process.* Between running a busy private practice and juggling three active children, she spends most of her free time on the sidelines watching sports or in the Rocky Mountains hiking, doing yoga, or snowboarding.

INDEX

Index

Find fulfillment at home and at work with the HBR Working Parents Series

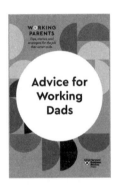

An all-in-one resource for every working parent.

If you enjoyed this book and want more guidance on working parenthood, turn to *Workparent: The Complete Guide to Succeeding on the Job, Staying True to Yourself, and Raising Happy Kids*. Written by Daisy Dowling, a top executive coach, talent expert, and working mom, *Workparent* provides all the advice and assurance you'll need to combine children and career in your own, authentic way.

AVAILABLE IN PAPERBACK
OR EBOOK FORMAT.